Manjits
AND THE
TANDOOR OF
SECRETS

Manjits
AND THE
TANDOOR OF SECRETS

First published in 2022 by Pepper Press,
an imprint of Fair Play Publishing
PO Box 4101, Balgowlah Heights, NSW 2093, Australia
www.pepperpress.com.au

ISBN: 978-1-925914-28-3
ISBN: 978-1-925914-29-0 (ePub)
© Michael Cain 2022

The moral rights of the author have been asserted.

All rights reserved. Except as permitted under the Australian Copyright Act 1968 (for example, a fair dealing for the purposes of study, research, criticism or review), no part of this book may be reproduced, stored in a retrieval system, communicated or transmitted in any form or by any means without prior written permission from the Publisher.

Cover photography by Steven Reinhardt
Manjits food photography by Dorota Grabowska-Kulka
Cover design by Ashley Reynolds
Internal Design and Typesetting by Leslie Priestley

All inquiries should be made to the Publisher via
sales@fairplaypublishing.com.au

A catalogue record of this book is available from the National Library of Australia.

Contents

Foreword by Kapil Dev — ix

Introduction — 1

PART 1: CULTURE — 5
- Leap of Faith: Leaving India — 6
- Browning out Racism — 14
- An Elephant in the Room — 18

PART 2: CONFLICT — 25
- Butter Chicken — 26
- Howzat for a Drama — 33
- Countering Covid — 38

PART 3: CUSTOMERS — 45
- Nearly Taking One for the Team — 46
- Celebs — 50
- Some Like It Hot — 56

MANJITS AND THE TANDOOR OF SECRETS

EPILOGUE	**61**
RECIPES FROM THE GUJRALS	**65**
Something My Parents Made	
Palak Paneer	67
Mixed Vegetable Jalfrezi	71
Something the Grandkids Love	
Vegetable Samosa	75
The Family Heirloom	
Butter Chicken – The Traditional Way	79
Butter Chicken – The Modern Spin	85
Our Best Seller	
Tandoori Chicken	87
Something Indians Always Order	
Classic Kadai Chicken	91
Something non-Indians Always Order	
South Indian Fish Curry	95
Balmain's Most Popular Dish	
Balmain Bug Curry	99
Something Gentler	
Lamb Korma	103
Something So Good	
Bharrah Kebab	107

Favourites

Manjit – **Goat Shoulder Curry**	111
Kawal – **Fish Amritsari**	115
Deep – **Yellow Dal**	119
Varun – **Duck Curry**	123

Something To Finish

Dhokla	127
Shahi Tukda	131
Galub Jamun	135

EXTRAS (THE BASICS)   139

Masala Curry Sauce	141

WEIGHTS AND MEASURES   145
ACKNOWLEDGEMENTS   146
ABOUT THE AUTHOR   147

Foreword by Kapil Dev

In life we are lucky to find people we can grow with. I am fortunate to have Manjit.

We grew up together, living in homes opposite each other. Then he left the country to make something of himself abroad.

To me, the final success isn't as important as the struggles he faced getting there. Now once that success is attained, everything feels so worth it.

Manjit is respected, appreciated and looked up to in the community, in India and Australia.

It is also lovely to see his children enjoy their father's success, but to continue it, they must remember his hard work.

I wish Manjit and his wife Kawal, who is an important part of his journey, all the very best.

I hope you enjoy learning more about their family in this beautiful book.

Kapil Dev
August 2022

Introduction

When I first heard of the Gujrals - Manjit, Kawal and sons Deep and Varun - writing about this successful Indian family wasn't on the radar.

At the time I was working in Sydney's Channel 10 newsroom and dabbled in the occasional documentary series. I was in the middle of writing a story about the national rugby league when I was interrupted by cameraman Drew Tanti telling me he had a story for me. *Yeah, yeah,* I thought. I'd love a penny every time someone pitched, in their eyes, an unbelievable story.

"Mate, I just did a live cross for Studio 10 at an Indian restaurant and this family is batshit crazy," he laughed.

"Go on," I said.

"They're loud, funny and outrageous, right down your alley."

Drew knew me all too well. For the previous few years at the network, my forte was doing stories that were different to your usual, run-of-the-mill news yarns. I love people and their stories. A documentary series I put together on billionaires and how they'd made their fortune was received well and I was always keen to do more.

MANJITS AND THE TANDOOR OF SECRETS

Everyone has a story. Good, bad, ugly, self-made or rags to riches, whether they're well known or 'no names' in the world.

Drew mentioned this family's ancestors had invented Butter Chicken and that's when my ears pricked up. That's a notable mention which would have a great storyline.

He said they were keen to meet me and passed their contacts on.

After doing a little research I realised they'd already featured in a series for SBS Television called 'Turban Legend'.

What could I offer them that they hadn't already portrayed?

It seemed they were still keen to do something, as they had thought the fly on the wall production would be longer. The Gujrals were under the impression it would be of multiple episodes, but as things happen in the entertainment industry, changes to the format meant the weeks of filming would be squeezed into just a one hour show and not a three-part series as expected.

I thought I could maybe do their story justice by doing it better.

When meeting with Deep Gujral, who runs the business operations, and his marketing/PR consultant Ash Reynolds, I didn't really know what to expect. I arrived at their restaurant in the city, known as Manjits, as the sun drenched over the harbour. The beauty of the interior took me aback. No expense spared, I thought.

The enthusiasm and humour both Deep and Ash showed in the first five minutes of the meeting made me immediately think there's a brilliant story here.

"We have a great story to tell," said Deep. "We are the Kardashians of the Indian restaurant scene. Our family is different to any family you're likely to ever meet, but we still make it work."

That sentence works for me. It usually meant "good television". Expect the unexpected—but I still worried about the fact SBS had beaten me to the punch. Editing a documentary can be punishing with time restraints and restrictions. You want everything in it without cutting good stuff out.

The tales that I have put together here come from speaking with the family, Ash, and other staff. I hope they give a glimpse of the family's entrepreneurism, creativity, showmanship, kindness, occasional madness, generosity and professionalism. I have attempted to share snippets of their fascinating lives as a family of Indian business owners in Australia.

Also included are recipes from the menus at the eponymous silver service restaurant Manjits Wharf in the city of Sydney, as well as at their function centre in suburban Concord, including some of their personal favourites.

I hope you enjoy the read. You most certainly will enjoy the recipes!

PART 1

Culture

The Gujrals are an Indian family, and no matter how long they live in Australia, they will always be that. Their roots and culture are deep within their hearts and memories, from how they cook to how they live their day to day lives. Unfortunately, along with this amazing melding of culture comes a downside: a cultural bias from some toward the colour of their skin. Good or bad, culture is everything to the Gujrals, and they are proud.

Leap of Faith: Leaving India

Backing your instinct can be a gutsy endeavour, especially when starting a new life in a new land.

Manjit and Kawal Gujral left India in 1983 with their two-year-old son, Deep, on the urging of Manjit's father, Makhan who had arrived in Australia two years earlier. Manjit's two brothers, Amar and Surjeet, had also made the same journey - Amar in 1974 and Surjeet in 1981 - and had already established an Indian restaurant in Sydney.

In India, Manjit worked as a sales executive for Blue Star, an Indian multinational home appliances company. It was a well-paid position, managing a team of fifty-five people. It was a job he enjoyed but it wasn't his passion.

As much as the move to a new country was exciting, a dose of reality hit on the first day, which had him questioning his decision.

Manjit was working on a food stall for one of his brothers on a hot day at Sydney's Royal Easter Show. He was in charge of heating and selling samosas, while sweeping and mopping the floor in between sales. It wasn't the best start. He felt like he had taken a backward step. Manjit explains:

"It was depressing. After working so hard to get where I was back in India,

this was a reality check. Kawal was in tears saying, "let's go back". This was not the type of work I was expecting. I wanted to go back home as well.

Then I said, "If I go back, what face would I show in India?" I became so emotional but couldn't bring myself to jump on the next flight home. My pride won out. I'm good at grasping things and once I jumped in the lake I had to swim and get to the other side."

After coming home late one night exhausted and smelling of sweat, Manjit knew he had to change tack. Instead of being a labourer for others, he decided he wanted to be the man calling the shots.

The next day he decided he would follow in his family's footsteps and learn how to cook.

But mastering traditional Indian recipes isn't an art form you can learn in just five minutes. For months, Manjit worked closely with his brothers, writing down every recipe, as well as learning the art of hospitality.

He unlocked the secrets of how to create a soft and buttery naan. He learned the right mix of spices for a Lamb Korma. He learned how to properly marinate Tandoori Chicken, while even finding the best way of using a deep saucepan that gives an even temperature for the best Rogan Josh.

It wasn't long before Manjit was earning his stripes in the extended family group, but it was also becoming increasingly difficult for three sets of families to survive with what was essentially one source of income.

Manjit and Kawal decided to strike out on their own. The decision to go it alone initially caused an argument between siblings, but they also knew the leap of faith had to be taken.

They found small premises in Potts Point in Sydney. Within months of arriving, they opened their first restaurant. They were on their way.

Not long after, Manjit and Kawal decided to find somewhere slightly larger and where the rent and outgoings would be less expensive than Sydney's eastern suburbs. A real estate agent who was a friend of Manjit's suggested premises in Balmain which had become available but warned the couple that it needed some work.

'Needing some work' was an understatement. When they first saw it, Kawal thought they had arrived at the wrong venue. Dirt and dust as far as the eye could see, broken old chairs that didn't even match, and a cooktop that looked as though it had never seen a cleaning agent.

However, despite the eyesore, they both instantly knew this was 'it'. They looked past what was before their eyes and into their future.

Within weeks, the business was up and running. Second-hand chairs and tables were sourced that matched the blue and gold colour scheme Kawal had designed. Before long, lunchtime specials were a big hit amongst the local Darling Street crowd, and regular customers kept the cash flow positive.

As Manjit cooked, Kawal ran the floor. It was a team effort, and they loved every minute, even the long hours which came with the territory.

Both Manjit and Kawal believe it was the best time of their business and, other than their two sons, their proudest achievement—starting with nothing yet making it work, while also raising a family.

The birth of their second son Varun in 1987 soon took focus for Kawal as the business kept booming. Manjit worked even longer hours in the restaurant while Kawal spent more time at home with the boys.

> "We loved what we were doing," Manjit explains. "There was a real vibe. It's like we were getting accepted in the community because of our cooking. It was hard work, especially with two young sons but we were slowly but surely getting there."

As the business grew, the opportunity to buy their first house became just as satisfying as anything the couple had achieved. Bricks and mortar were a real statement. It meant the leap of faith to leave India was justified. Manjit nearly kissed the real estate agent on the day the house keys were handed over. Only five years earlier, the thought of leaving the only place they knew to half a world away would have been considered a crazy notion.

Manjit and Kawal put plenty of hours and elbow grease into their first solo venture, which became the oldest running Indian restaurant in Australia until they leased it out in December 2020.

After the first year of the COVID-19 pandemic, and together with the flagship eponymous restaurant in the city, the function centre in suburban Concord, and the pre-prepared packaged business, something had to give for the Gujrals. For Kawal, it was like losing an arm. The Balmain shop was still making a profit, but everyone was stretched in different directions.

Back then, Kawal believes Manjit's stubbornness, which at times frustrates her, was the key to their early success. He set a goal and he stuck to it.

For Kawal the new lifestyle in Australia had its own challenges but it was a blessing in disguise. A new sense of independence wasn't lost on her.

Growing up in the agricultural city of Sri Ganganagar in the Indian state of Rajasthan, she vividly remembers the family cow that used to roam the house and provide milk for everyone. Chipping in with the family unit to help prepare feasts is also a vivid memory as much as the strong odour of dried, brittle red chillies, which would make her eyes water as she ground them into a paste with cumin, onions, garlic, and coriander on a grinding stone.

For some young girls living in rural India, the transition from childhood and adolescence to womanhood has many cultural and social controls. There is a belief that a woman's primary role is that of a caregiver. Many feel they're destined to get married and do kitchen work only. Some feel trapped in the knowledge they'll eventually have an arranged marriage and conform to parental expectations.

MANJITS AND THE TANDOOR OF SECRETS

People learn the essential themes of cultural life within the bosom of the family. In most of the country, the basic units of society are the patrilineal family unit and wider kinship groupings. The large, extended family is commonplace, generally comprising three or four related generations, all living under one roof, eating, working, worshipping, and cooperating in social and economic activities.

In this environment, parents traditionally are domineering, making choices about careers and marriage for their children. While the practice of arranged marriages dates back thousands of years, it remains commonplace in many parts of the world, especially in India.

The kinship system, particularly among Hindus in the North, is strongly tied to arranged marriages which sustains the patrilineal and patrilocal family system.

Sikh marriage is known as an 'Anand Karaj' means a 'Ceremony of Bliss'. Sikh families such as those of Manjit and Kawal also accept the idea of an assisted or arranged marriage, which is not the same as a forced marriage as both the son and daughter have a choice about whether they want to wed.

At the age of twenty-two, Kawal's folks started approaching their extended family and friend networks to find a prospective groom. When Manjit turned up, Kawal admits it wasn't love at first sight.

"I had to respect the family's wishes. I toed the traditional line. I didn't feel weird because you just think it's normal, which it is in many parts of India. I remember the night Manjit turned up at the house. He was polite and shy and so was I, which made it even harder to communicate. I fell in love with Manjit over a few months. Our life has been one big experience and we couldn't be happier."

Now when Kawal goes back to visit India she sees young women that are in a similar situation to herself decades before, waiting for the next step in their life. She says that Australia has given her freedom and choice which she would not have enjoyed in her homeland.

MANJITS AND THE TANDOOR OF SECRETS

Kawal believes women are looking for intellect and someone who is on the same wavelength, while parents are focused on wealth. Nonetheless, she still believes there is a small silver lining in an arranged marriage as it can also at times 'cut to the chase'. Parents know their kids best and finding someone with similar interests can make things easier. Concentrating on whether love will form, rather than worrying about compatibility, can save a lot of hassle in the courtship.

Women do ultimately have a choice over their prospective mates but they still feel pressured to get married.

> "It's not like you have to do it," Kawal says. "It is more like, you please the parents but if it's not going to work, then that's it. You don't go ahead. In saying that, some families would push hard to change minds, this is despite the big changes and modernisation India has undergone in the seventy years since independence."

Deep argues that people using the dating service 'Tinder' and similar apps and websites are engaging in something similar to an arranged marriage process.

> "You're essentially picking what you want. Is there much of a difference? It's just that your parents aren't doing it for you. You get to pick the nationality, skin colour, smile, etcetera, and go on a date."

The forty-year marriage between Kawal and Manjit has been built on faith and trust. You still see it between them as they continue to live and love each other.

Kawal's practical upbringing is a big part of the success of the business. Put simply, Kawal is the glue that holds it all together. When a fight breaks out between the males, she is the voice of reason, who douses the flames and brokers peace between the opposing parties.

As the Gujral sons get older, they realise more and more just how much their parents have sacrificed for the family.

For Varun, it was his paternal grandmother who also played a part in his future direction. Her babysitting created his zest for cooking as he went from playing with toys to helping his grandmother prepare meals in the home kitchen.

> "She was an amazing woman. I would get up and she would be cooking pancakes, which is why I was a fat child. I helped her prepare spices, some of the dishes she'd prepare had thirty to forty spices in each one. She was the reason I decided cooking was for me."

In those years Varun went from watching cartoons to being transfixed by cooking shows. He was even experimenting with food in the family kitchen and pleading with his father to take him to the restaurant, a request Manjit always refused.

Education was an important part of the pair's upbringing, and Deep now looks back with regret that he didn't study harder considering the sacrifice made by his parents to put them into a top private school.

Both men's occupation of choice is a world apart from what they're currently involved in. Varun wanted to be a lawyer, Deep a pilot, although now he's into MMA fighting. Yes, you read correctly. It his way of escaping. the madness of a high-pressure business.

While their own men, Deep and Varun are also different versions of Manjit. One is the passionate and organised businessman. The other is a devoted and creative chef. The influence and support of their strong mother is noticeable. In Manjit's words, "she understands the psychology of all three of us."

Kawal, to her own admission, is the referee and has witnessed some heated exchanges. Disagreements will continue to play out within the group and chaos will still reign as the business continues to expand.

As challenging and dysfunctional as it may seem for four members of a family to work so closely together, somehow it still works. The engine room may look like a madhouse behind the scenes, but the delivery stays seamless as the four pull together when it counts.

Whether in business or in their personal life they have each other's back.

For two proud parents who took a punt on a new life all those years ago, the best recipe they created has been their own family.

Browning out Racism

As a 5-year-old Indian boy
walked towards the rusty old entrance
gates holding his mother's hand
for his first day of school, plenty was
going on in his mind.

Other kids in the exact same uniform stared at him, making him uncomfortable and he couldn't work out why. Maybe they couldn't wait to become friends with him and play? Could it be the Spiderman thermos flask and matching lunch box he had picked out at the shops the previous day? They might be envious.

Never in his mind did he think it was because his skin was a different colour, and because he wore a patka—a head covering worn by Sikh children in preference to a turban. It keeps hair manageable. It is made from cloth and knotted at the top. It was the knotted top itself which caused questions and insults.

To Deep, all the other pupils were just like him. They wore the same clothes, had the same oversized backpacks.

By recess, he was made aware he was different. Kids can be cruel at the best of times, but this was torture.

MANJITS AND THE TANDOOR OF SECRETS

The interrogation began. Why are you black and why have you got a stupid beanie on?

Deep couldn't answer either question. He himself thought, 'they're right. Why am I a different colour and why haven't they got a patka on top of their heads?'

'Why have you got a tennis ball stuck to your head?'

'Is that your second head?'

'You look stupid.'

For Deep, it couldn't get any worse.

> "It was my first day of school in Australia and the old man makes me wear a turban! It put a target on my back! I don't remember anything else from that first day at school apart from the nastiness. I couldn't learn anything. I was shitting myself through the lessons, worrying about recess, worrying about lunch, even worried my mother would be late to pick me up after school because I'd cop it then too.
>
> "They used to pull the bun at the top, which meant the wrapping fell apart and with no one there at the school who knew how to fix it, it left me distraught. After a fortnight my mum took me to the hairdressers to get my hair cut to end the misery. I couldn't contain my excitement on the way but when we got there the barbershop had closed for the day. I cried and cried."

As the years went on, Deep eventually went to one of Sydney's elite private boys' schools, but the racist taunts didn't stop. They got more personal.

Curry-muncher. Raghead. Terrorist. Monkey Boy.

It cut to the bone, but by his teens, Deep had built an armour. Instead of crying to Kawal, Manjit, or the teachers, he gave it back. But in a witty way. Not a racist taunt or slant. Deep had an answer for every derogatory comment designed to make the perpetrator look stupid. If in a group situation, the group would turn on the bully.

In 2019, an incident on the other side of the world caused Deep to remember the patka incident when he was child.

Captain Simranjeet Gujral, a Sikh pilot for India's national carrier Air India claims he was asked to remove his turban for manual inspection at airport security in Madrid. It had Shiromani Akali leader Manjinder Singh Sirsa seeing red, tweeting, "He was subjected to racial discrimination because of his Turban. The Turban is the essence of Sikh identity, and it is important to create awareness at the global level about how sensitive Sikhs are about their turban."

Racism comes in many different ways, and via many different people. Australia is no exception, and has been in the spotlight in recent years.

Savage attacks in 2010 on Indian students in Melbourne saw widespread protests in the community that resulted in student enrolment numbers plummet. The racially motivated attacks were significant enough for then Prime Minister Kevin Rudd to apologise and try to mend diplomatic relations by making a dash to India and later setting up the Australia India Institute.

Ten years later in the midst of the COVID-19 pandemic, Australia's threat to jail citizens returning home from India sparked outrage, with some critics labelling the measure as racist and a breach of human rights.

Even now, nearly all of Deep's Australian friends will accidentally say things that he knows is racist, but they don't realise it. Like the time his mates went to a café and ordered scones and jam. "Do you know what a scone is?" asked a mate.

"Ummm, isn't that a muffin or a type of bread," Deep responds in his dumb voice. Followed up by, "Of course I know what a friggin' scone is. I'm Indian, not stupid!"

The fact Deep can now laugh at the racial demons which once haunted him is testimony to how far he's come as a person.

When I first met Deep, he showed me two pictures in his Concord office. Both images were of Manjit employees, one at the Concord Function Centre, the other at the restaurant in Sydney's CBD.

"What do you see out of both of those?" he said. At first, I just saw about twenty people all smiling at the camera. "Look closer," he urged. The penny then dropped. The function centre staff are all white-skinned and the fine dining restaurant were dark-skinned.

Deep then explained the reason behind it.

> *"Look, Indians can be racist too. We talk about discrimination against us but look at the caste system. Why we set it up in two different ways is that predominately we cater for Indian weddings. So, to keep the peace we have Australian staff. If we had Indians manning the tables, there would be no end of trouble throughout the night. Sad but true. Even sober, some Indians will look down at waiters and waitresses. Serve alcohol to them and it gets twenty times worse. You can see it straight away at an event. When someone puts their hand in the air and clicks their fingers to get attention, I find it rude and insulting. Like they're saying, 'where is my servant?' You have to just suck it up though. Remember, these nights cost hundreds of thousands of dollars. And we're in the hospitality game. It goes with the territory."*

Deep explained that the fine-dining restaurant sees all nationalities come through the doors. Many are white.

> *"Australians expect to be served by an Indian in an Indian restaurant. They want the Indian experience. A good example is our two different butter chickens, both traditional and modern are popular but to two different crowds. Aussies want traditional, Indians want modern."*

An Elephant in the Room

Across the globe, culture varies in many ways. It encompasses, beliefs, values, food, laws, music, arts, marriage, dress, sport, and traits of religious, racial, or social groups.

India's cultures are as diverse as it comes. Cultural diversity exists, but there are also common themes across all cultural groups.

In the food and catering business, acceptance of all cultures is vital.

"Sometimes for example, a Muslim bride might be marrying a Sikh groom," Kawal explains.

"Catering for this must be delicate as Muslims don't drink alcohol, while Sikhs do. Just setting out the room is hard, but you can't simply draw a line down the middle. We look to create inclusiveness and we want the night to go smoothly because on many occasions this will be the first time both sets of families meet. If they get off to a bad start, it can usually stay that way. I think we have a lot of responsibility to help make it a good start."

One aspect of culture that is close to the heart of the family's matriarch is art. A keen painter, Kawal spends many hours pouring her thoughts onto a canvas, mostly in bright, vibrant colours. She says it's her escape from her work life.

Because some of the world's major religions such as Hinduism, Buddhism, and Islam began or flourished in India, many of India's artworks are based on political or religious subject matter.

But for Kawal, it's purely just a passionate pastime.

"The main aim is to create beauty and while working on a painting, I keep that in mind. Indian arts have a strong position around the world. As compared to other forms of art like music and dance, paintings portray the emotions and feelings of the artist for a very long time. I probably don't get as much time these days to paint, which is strange at this stage of my life. You'd think things would have slowed down for us, but it's the other way around."

Ceremony is also an essential part of culture. Knowing the wide variations of culture and religion both inside and outside of India is a fine art, and one that Deep has had to learn on the job.

One example is the Korean Paebaek ceremony. The Paebaek ceremony is an intimate Korean unification tradition historically performed after the main wedding ceremony to symbolise the entrance of the bride into her husband's household. The ceremony features Korean historical traditions like formal bowing, a tea ceremony, and the couple catching chestnuts and dates.

At one point, the groom's parents sit behind the table in front of a backdrop of natural scenery. Once the groom's parents are situated, the attendant will alert the couple to enter and bow in the direction of the groom's parents. The bride's bow differs from the groom's bow as well as the guests' bows.

Deep explains, "You need to know the cultural component of what they do. Sometimes clients are surprised I know a lot of this. There's a lot of bowing but that's their tradition and we have to have some understanding of it for it all to work on the day."

Traditional culture also doesn't come without its trials.

Deep prides himself on delivering whatever type of demand comes across his desk, but this request was nearly beyond his capabilities. The couple wanted him to find an elephant for a baraat—the groom's wedding procession—which proved to be more than a little problematic.

Finding an elephant to use at an event isn't as simple as calling the nearest zoo and asking if one can be rented for a few hours. In saying that, Deep did email Sydney's Taronga Zoo to request this, but unsurprisingly he never received a reply.

Most families, both in the past and present, use horses for their baraat, but this family wanted to go all out.

The ceremony was at a Sikh Temple and had a gathering of over six hundred people. Given the astounding amount of money both families were willing to spend, it's no surprise that impressing the guests was the aim.

"Although it's uncommon, riding an elephant into a wedding reception is not unheard of," Deep said. "But where do you get an elephant from in Australia? You can't just go down to your local 7-Eleven and pick one up. I searched far and wide. I called on nearly every contact I had in my black book to track one down. I was about to give up."

Finally, though, his persistence paid off.

A friend from India sent a message that an adult female elephant named Bimbi was available in the town of Esperance in Western Australia. The animal's owner was hesitant at first, wanting to know exactly what was required of his pet. Despite the hesitance, Deep struck a five-figure deal with the owner—and then the next dilemma arose.

How was the four thousand kilogram beast going to be transported 3,500 kilometres across Australia?

It had started as a bit of fun, but this experience was starting to engulf the whole job. Deep felt he was taking his eye off the ball in other areas of the job and was worried he had let down clients.

A transport company that normally caters to horses was brought in. It was another big expense, but at this stage Deep didn't care—he'd gone too far to turn back. Not getting too many bookings to move an exotic animal, the receptionist thought it was a prank call at first. Bimbi's owner also demanded to be flown to Sydney and accommodated, to be close to the action.

The day finally came when the elephant needed to be placed on a truck for the long trip. In addition to the owner, an elephant handler called Dulep was also recruited to travel with the animal to make sure it was a stress-free trip.

Loading Bimbi on the truck wasn't easy, but once she was on board she settled in nicely. Dulep demanded the truck stopped every fifty kilometres to check on Bimbi.

The slow trip became even slower once the vehicle arrived in Adelaide. Animal rights group PETA (People for the Ethical Treatment of Animals) wanted to see all the paperwork involved.

Deep recalls, "It took me nearly two days to get the paperwork required for them. It meant we had to house Bimbi while the journey ground to a halt. I get what they do, it was just tough. Don't worry about the elephant's stress levels, mine was through the roof!"

Once in Sydney, Bimbi was taken to horse racing track, Rosehill Gardens, where she was accommodated until the big day. All the time, she had to be fed and watered with a sponge bath thrown in daily.

Even though the logistics were taken care of, the work continued for Deep as he sought permission to close a street for an elephant to walk down, searched for public liability insurance, worried about purchasing the correct food for an elephant, and located someone at the ready to pick up Bimbi's poo. To say it was an ordeal is an understatement—especially the last requirement. Elephants defecate between twelve to fifteen times per day, a daily quantity of 100-115 kilograms. That particular job was outsourced as Manjits' staff, who are normally willing to do anything, gave it a wide berth.

Negotiating with the local council was also a slow affair. Streets needed to be booked to stop traffic. Deep explains, "It was like moving heaven and earth. If I had known it was going to be so hard, I'd have said no right from the get-go. We've had fireworks, ice sculptures, sports cars, you name it. We've just about done it when it comes to wedding celebrations, but this one was so draining."

The big day came and it was all systems go.

Dressed in a beautiful red and gold fabric and delivered to the site, Bimbi was a showstopper. People in cars were slowing down to look at a this amazingly rare spectacle – an elephant parading through the streets of suburban Sydney. Others were taking selfies, as a big crowd started to gather.

Deep thought he was getting an experienced animal when it came to working with crowds, but another surprise was in store when he found out on the day it was, in fact, Bimbi's first public appearance as an adult elephant.

This was discovered only when they realised that Bimbi was making weird noises as she was taken out of her crate. The sound of horns from impatient drivers spooked her to the point of nearly charging down a busy street.

"Surely she's used to vehicles going past," said Deep to the trainer as a statement rather than a question.

"No. This is her first time in this environment," came the reply from Dulep.

Deep groaned. "Jesus Christ. You'll have her killed or someone else killed or twenty cars destroyed if we're not careful."

At this point, Deep chose to go back inside the reception. He figured out of sight, out of mind—but a smell stopped him in his tracks. Looking down, he discovered that while he was discussing the elephant with the attendant, Bimbi had rather inelegantly dirtied down the side of Deep's cream-coloured trouser leg and onto his white, leather shoes.

As Deep said, "It typified everything about the whole process from start to finish."

The procession started and, despite loud drums banging close to her, Bimbi never faltered from the job at hand as her enormous legs slowly moved towards the temple.

The convoluted process was finished after twenty metres. Yes, Bimbi only had to walk twenty metres and her job was done. Even then, it wasn't over for Deep, who then had the task of getting Bimbi back over to Western Australia.

Was it worth it?

The bride and groom certainly thought so. Both sets of parents did, too. But for Deep who made it all happen, the sight of an elephant makes him break out into a cold sweat every time.

PART 2

Conflict

The thing about families is that they argue. Things go wrong. People make mistakes, and the rest of the family have to be there to look after them and back them up. That's the way it is, always has been, and probably always will be—and the way it should be. Not only that, but outside forces always loom on the horizon, waiting to strike and ruin everything if the family and business can't remain strong. For the Gujrals, who live and work and surround themselves with each other day in day out, this is clearer than for anyone. But it's through these conflicts, and these mistakes, that they flourish.

Butter Chicken

Whether it be by accident, design or re-invention, creating a dish that stands the test of time and is consumed the world over is no easy feat.

The Mexicans have the Taco – thought to originate either in the 16th or 19th centuries. The French invented crepes. The Italians have pasta. The Hungarians have goulash. And the Koreans have kimchi.

Ancestors of the Gujrals created a dish that's as famous as it gets when it comes to Punjabi cuisine.

Butter Chicken's history has its family name written all over it and just like the taco and pasta, it has seen slight changes over the years. It is the newest version of the famed dish by Varun that saw him nearly come to blows with Manjit.

Tandoori Chicken, the parent dish of Butter Chicken, was born 100 years ago in Gora Bazaar in Peshawar, where a man named Mokha Singh Lamba started a small restaurant. The kitchen's young chef Kundan Lai Gujral thought he'd experiment by skewering yogurt marinated pieces of chicken and putting them into the tandoor, which was previously used for bread only. It was cooked in the heat of the clay tandoor, which was flavoured by the smoke rising from the hot coals created a crispy skin and an unmistakable bright red exterior.

The new dish became popular with many, until Kundan was forced to flee Pakistan during the 1947 Partition of India. He fled to Delhi with his family to try their luck at an abandoned restaurant in Daryaganj, which was considered a newer part of Old Delhi. The new establishment was formed with a partner, Thakur Das Mago and they called it 'Moti Mahal'. Word traveled fast and it didn't take long before the modest eatery lined with sandstone was getting repeat business.

The refrigeration facilities or lack thereof at the time led Kundan to innovate yet again to avoid wastage of unsold tandoori tikkas.

He decided to add a tomato gravy with butter and cream that would soften the leftover chicken, which he would then sell to the lunchtime crowd. The combination proved to be a masterstroke and thus by accident or an act of genius, 'Butter Chicken' was born.

In the 1970s, Kundal Lal's son, Nand Lal Gujral joined the partnership and helped establish the Moti Mahal Delux Chain of Restaurants. Indian leaders like Jawahar Lal Nehru, Indira Gandhi, Zakir Husain, and many foreign dignitaries have visited Moti Mahal to sample the innovations of Kundal Lal and Nand Lal Gujral.

Despite Butter Chicken becoming hugely popular for westerners, Indian clientele seldom order it.

At Manjits' eateries, it is more of a hit with kids at the many functions they cater for.

"Aussies take it like a drug," Varun laughs. "It is on the menu at many places in India but it's certainly not the 'go-to' dish. They like spicy dishes and Butter Chicken does not fall into that category.

This recipe has caused a divide in the family's cooking ranks, with Manjit and Varun in opposite corners. Varun's ear is constantly being chewed by his dad on how menus, which in some cases take weeks to conjure up, should stay traditional. Varun enjoys putting his own spin on them, often coming up with infusing modern elements into the Indian cuisine.

"I was stuck doing the same butter chicken recipe in the Balmain restaurant. I felt like I was working with handcuffs on. Especially in that community, people just didn't want change. If you try to make a change or take something off the menu, people would want to know why. Butter chicken is a butter chicken – you can't play around with it. If you go to McDonald's to get a Big Mac it's got to be the same every day."

The day came when Varun presented his new look version of Manjit's historic, pride and joy. He served it on individual plates using a whole chicken breast, Kyiv-style, accompanied by a mixed vegetable spicy jalfrezi and spicy tomato mash.

Manjit sat stunned for a few minutes looking, at what he thought, barely resembled his ancestor's famous dish. His face turned as red as the tie and matching turban he was wearing. His idea on food is to eat with your eyes first, smell second and taste third and on this occasion, his eyes were not happy.

Manjit's view was if the wheels aren't broken why change?

"You know what I think? You've served up disrespect," he roared while angrily unbuttoning his blazer. "It doesn't look like butter chicken, so don't even bother putting it on."

The Gujral's marketing and PR consultant, Ash Reynolds, sat in on the meeting and chimed in: "Manjit, why don't you taste it and decide?" If looks could kill, Ash would be six-feet under. From that point Ash kept quiet.

Varun, now clearly agitated, decided to state his case. "Let's be movers and shakers in this industry. This is an example of what I can do and what I want to do. I don't want to make just good food, I want to make crave-able food."

"By destroying a signature dish? Is that being a mover and shaker?" Manjit fired back.

"This is non-negotiable. The old Butter Chicken stays. I'll be a laughing stock in India if this happens. I don't want to talk about it anymore. If you don't like it, leave. Everyone's replaceable."

He then got up from the table, knocking over a jug of water in the process before racing out the front doors.

Ash looked at Varun. "Well, that went well." he said, expecting at least a smile.

"I've had it, I'm done. I'll start my own f...ing restaurant," was the reply.

Looking back, Varun can see how it would have offended his dad. He knows there's a place on the menu for the classics, but from his perspective, he also wanted space for a point of difference. At the time he was also struggling with the boredom of being a chef and doing the same things every day, and he wanted to branch out into new menus.

"There are days when I feel I just can't do it anymore. There are times I think, get me out of this industry. I'd do anything. Anything. I'll go uber-ing, I don't care. But the strange thing is, when I stop or whenever I have a rest, I get enthused to want to go again. It's like a mistress. It just lures you back in and you fall in love with it all over again."

The disastrous meeting with dad resulted in Varun choosing to push ahead with an adventurous career move he had in mind for some while. After alluding he may quit the family business, Varun decided to help a friend that was involved with a community bowling club in Sydney's north shore. At the time , the club was struggling to find a caterer.

Most licensed clubs sub-lease their bistro area and the ones that don't, employ fulltime catering staff, which usually see cooks come and go, mainly due to being poached to work elsewhere for better money.

Varun saw this as the perfect time to spread his wings and show the rest of the family he is more than a chef.

To get this to happen he had to get it over the line with the club's board of directors, and Varun knew the very person who could give his pitch every chance to be delivered professionally with no stone unturned. That person was Ash.

For Ash, it was one big nightmare. His duties looking after Manjits Wharf as well as the function centre had suddenly expanded overnight to include a suburban bowling club. All of his regular responsibilities were put on hold for almost three weeks in an effort to put the best proposal together for Varun's entrepreneurial dream becoming a reality.

A proposal was prepared that included everything from re-branding the club, renaming the new bistro 'Chatties', data on the residents who lived in the area (average age and income), and an environmental and sustainability commitment. The problem Ash faced was that Varun and his friend and new-found business partner had already promised the world in an informal meeting with several club directors weeks earlier.

One of those promises was to use the 'Manjits' name in the new kitchen, which he believed would attract new members. However, this wasn't discussed with Manjit himself and once it was brought up in a family chat, it was a flat-out "no". Manjit thought that an association with a bowling club was inconsistent with the brand.

Despite this setback from Varun's point-of-view, the bowling club's Board unanimously voted for Varun to become boss of the new enterprise.

Making a new menu was one of the biggest challenges, as it was important not to make it an all-Indian menu. Hamburgers, chicken schnitzel, and chips go hand in hand at most venues like this, so this was really branching out for Varun in a new way.

It also meant dividing his time between the restaurant and the club, a balancing act that was never going to be simple. He was excited about the task ahead. He felt like this could spawn into something even bigger, which if done right, could encompass more clubs. His family, on the other hand, were not enthusiastic and the venture was met with a great deal of scepticism.

MANJITS AND THE TANDOOR OF SECRETS

The family relented because they realised Varun would probably find a way to do it anyway, with or without their blessing.

Although the food was made in Manjits' kitchen, it wasn't branded. A delivery van took the Indian food to the site, while the rest of the menu was made in-house at the bowling club. For a while, people came. The word got out that the food was from the swank place in the city, and some locals loved the change from eating chicken schnitzel and fish and chips to Beef Vindaloo and Lamb Korma.

Varun got a kick out of turning up and seeing bums on seats regardless of what food was going in their mouths. But to keep everything running like clockwork required Kawal. She spent hours driving, delivering and often working late at the bowling club, supporting her son. But she was run off her feet and something had to give.

For Varun, the business was like a shiny new toy, but as the novelty wore off, so did Varun's presence in the establishment and promises made in the proposal were not being delivered. The Board became restless; so 13 months after shaking hands on a deal, Varun quietly withdrew.

Varun realised that burning the candle at both ends came at a cost. Branching-out by himself was an itch Varun needed and wanted to scratch. Maybe he bit off more than he could chew, but it gave him a greater insight as to why and how the dynamics of the family business works.

With more time on his hands, Varun gave more thought to how to refine a new Butter Chicken pitch to his father. After Manjit's reaction the first time - which he thought was an over-reaction - he realised this was his last shot.

This time Manjit was prepared to listen. He, too, felt he may have gone over the top in the first attempt, but he was not prepared to show it, keeping his poker-face on.

After giving Varun a two-hour re-cap on their family history and its importance, a deal was struck to add the 'new look Butter Chicken' to the function centre menu, but the restaurant serving was strictly to remain as the original. The difference is not largely in the ingredients or the taste, but the way it is presented and served.

The decision by Manjit to allow Varun's version was a win for Varun in more ways than one. He felt like he had not disrespected his ancestors. In fact, he believes he took a punt and tried something different just like Kundal Gujral did all those years ago in New Delhi when he improvised.

So like the humble taco, pasta, or crepe, Butter Chicken lives on in its 'old' and 'new' guise and is eaten by people from all walks of life. Presidents to paupers and everyone in between.

It also meant a lot that his father gave him the chance, trusted him, and backed his judgment on something that's held dear to the family's heart. As a result, Varun now feels closer to Manjit than ever before.

In what would have been truly innovative if it had come off, there was almost a third creation of the dish, but it was never unleashed on the public after a family taste test.

The aim was to make a new dessert, which would attract headlines. As the trolley neared the table, Varun announced, "May I present to you Butter Chicken Sorbet!".

For Deep, it was an experiment that went too far. *"It was shit, wrapped in shit, wrapped in another layer of shit. Sometimes I swear he's trying to poison the lot of us. Now that would make headlines,"* he said with a smirk.

Howzat for a Drama

The fact the Gujral's have continued to be successful has a lot to do with the family's ability to ride drama to the other side.

No one knows this as much as Ash and Deep. They're good friends and talk often. They both have a good sense of when the business needs a fine-tune even when things are going smoothly. If a bad review comes in, a review into the bad review will be performed.

Sometimes it's a case of tough love, but Ash is family, and family sometimes gives tough love.

He says what he thinks but knows how hard to push Manjit. In saying this, Manjit is never very receptive to bad feedback, not that there's ever too much. More nit-picking stuff rather than food critique. Manjit usually bristles if someone complains. He feels like it's a case of he's made the effort to accommodate a customer's night and he did nothing to make a visitor feel unwelcome, so it is seen by him as a personal attack.

Another thing that seems to be a worldwide problem is the onslaught of scammers.

In the middle of the Indian national cricket team's 2020-21 tour of Australia, a scandal broke which saw Manjit's and the company's reputation come under fire. After winning the rights to cater for the team throughout their tour, Manjit was pleased as punch. To be able to feed the squad which so many people idolise is an honour beyond words for Manjit. Not only is the catering for all days of play but for all meals the squad required away from the ground.

Leading up to the tour, a person reached out to Deep, wanting to organise a meet and greet with the Indian cricket team in mid-January at the Darling Harbour restaurant. That time of year is the peak season for Manjits, but Deep thought the man on the other end of the phone was actually an official from the touring party.

After asking for pricing, an initial contract was signed and a deposit sent, but no face-to-face contact was made. Deep sent Ash a text message telling him of the event with the one-word reply "Brilliant" returned within seconds. A phone call to his father was next, knowing his love for celebrities frequenting the establishment.

"This is great news," yelled Manjit. "This will be a night to remember. The whole Indian team in our restaurant. This will make news back home, let me assure you."

It certainly did, but not the way Manjit was thinking.

Tickets sold for between $300-$500 a pop as the promoter used ads on social media and Gumtree to promote the night, as well as putting flyers on parked cars at the Sydney Cricket Ground during the last one-day international between the tourists and Australia.

Arrangements were made to roster more staff to cater for what would see over 200 people attend as the event promised to provide "amazing food, beer, wine and soft drink, fantastic interviews" with the Indian cricket team.

Varun, who had planned a holiday, was told he would have to ditch his plans which went down like a lead balloon. Deep didn't need an argument at this point as he knew it would go on forever. But their mum, Kawal, was already on the case and reasoned with Varun as to how this is a team effort and sacrifices have to be made at times.

Manjit was going to even throw more money into this as they knew it would attract media attention which would be good for business. The thought of asking his good friend and Indian cricket legend, Kapil Dev to come and MC the night was also on Manjit's mind.

The date was set just after the new year. Deep wanted to set up a meeting to speak to the organiser of the cricketer meet and greet in person to discuss decorating and timings—and that's when things started to unravel. After numerous emails, phone calls, and texts with no reply, he decided to reach out to Indian team management to get to the bottom of it.

Deep had connections with the Indian team management, as Manjits were catering for the team throughout the summer. His heart sunk when the team manager said neither he nor anyone else had any knowledge of the event.

"F…! I've been had," Deep thought.

Straight away he reported it to the police and the Australian Competition and Consumer Commission's ScamWatch service.

The fact that Manjits' name was being used to promote this night made Deep feel sick to the stomach. He called Ash who went straight into damage control. Scalping tickets isn't new in the sporting world but that's usually for games—not dinners.

A press release was issued within the hour, following which Deep started receiving phone calls from TV and Radio stations. It was the perfect opportunity to hammer the point that they were the innocent party.

Manjit's top priority was the reputation of the brand, and his concern was for the unwitting ticket holders who were under the impression that they were hours away from a hearty meal and meet and greet at his flagship venue.

"Deep, we'll have to call the guests and tell them that they're still welcome to come with their ticket and we'll at least give them a meal," Manjit proposed.

"We don't have their phone numbers, Dad, we don't have a guest list. All the sales have been made by this nutcase, and he has all their money and account details," Deep responded.

"I'll get up there and just tell it like it is. The authorities have been made aware and we can only do what we can do. No one will judge us for telling the truth."

In an interview with one of Australia's biggest morning shows, Deep said:

> "Our good name has come into disrepute, and we want to set the record straight. We had nothing to do with this. We know people have paid good money and may not get it back. What I can promise is that if people do turn up, we will cater for them in some capacity to honour their tickets.
>
> "Indian cricket team supporters and fans are predominately Indian, it's like a religion to them. And coupled with our brand and company, it's the perfect sort of atmosphere to meet and greet all these players. But it's a total scam. We're really disappointed. We've tried to get in contact with the fraudster, with the scam artist. However, he's dodged and weaved."

The interviews continued throughout the day talking to newspaper reporters and radio presenters on how it all unfolded, and he didn't miss a beat.

It had to be the perfect roll-out, and it was.

Building a good reputation over many years takes a lot of hard work and to think someone could rip that down from one act of greed would have been a tragedy. Now Deep looks harder at all events that are booked and demands seeing the person first before any type of contract is issued. Can you blame him?

The news did reach most Indian news services. Manjit thought his relatives would look at this with great shame but the feedback he got was positive. They had dealt with the potential fallout the only sensible way - on the front foot and telling the truth.

For the record, the planned night saw about a dozen people turn up to see if Deep would be true to his words. Their tickets were honoured, and they were all given a good meal and service.

Countering Covid

The horrible events which have transpired due to COVID-19 is something the family struggles to talk about. Their normal upbeat demeanour on everything in life disappeared.

Sorrow is a constant, as they think about the tragedy that has occurred, but there is also a feeling of gratitude in the backs of their mind.

The gratitude is also tempered by guilt because of a sense of helplessness. Seeing images of bodies being moved onto crates and subsequently lifted into backs of trucks from towns close to where both Manjit and Kawal grew up is unbearable viewing. They feel like there is every chance someone in that vision could be someone they know, while at the same time, praying it's not one of their own relatives.

The events of the 'COVID years' have made Manjit think back to many years ago when he was at the fork in the road of life. The direction he took may have indirectly saved him and his family's lives.

In terms of business, many of the Indian functions were disrupted due to guests whose lives have been affected by the turmoil in India. This is because the period of mourning is one year after a death, after which a family will observe a memorial event called 'sraddha' which pays homage to the deceased.

When the first case of the pandemic-bound coronavirus was identified in Australia in January 2020, the family could see the writing on the wall; they realised they would have to act fast to protect the business.

The discussions that followed were focused on how everyone could keep their jobs through what would become difficult times.

Weddings play a big part in their income stream and with long-term lockdowns being talked about, they needed to be on top of everything before the expected avalanche of enquiries poured in. Worried couples were anxious their big day was in jeopardy; some were worried about losing their deposit; others hoped for the best that things would recover quickly. Many questions simply couldn't be answered—not only did Deep and Ash not know, but everyone from the Prime Minister down was experiencing a pandemic and its impact for the first time in living memory.

It was the toughest period of Ash's business career.

> "We had to keep an eye on every government decision so we knew what we could do and couldn't do. I left that for Deep to handle because I needed to come up with a way to keep the kitchen churning and employees in a job. I also told him not to panic, that he would have to act 'Mr Cool' and not look like we were petrified. When I look back, I think we all were."

Keeping the kitchen going was vital for survival and creating takeaway delivery packs was the plan. This kept people employed and the function centre was used to put the idea into play. Social media was the way of telling people they were still in business.

The mantra was that 'people can't come to us, so we must come to the people'.

The venture struck an instant chord with many locked inside their homes. Ash says.

> "It was going crazy, there was so much demand for the packs. No one else was doing anything like this so early in the piece. It got to the point that Deep was contemplating hiring more staff to cater for it all."

As weeks went by, Deep says it went ballistic.

> "We were run off our feet, there was so much demand for the packs. It got to the point where I was going home more exhausted than normal. But it was a different type of exhaustion. More physical than mental. I was gone the minute my head hit the pillow."

Waiters, bar staff, function centre operators, and secretaries all became kitchen hands and delivery drivers. There was no real push back with the new roles. Everyone knew this was going to keep money coming in both to the business and to their households when so many others had neither.

Seven days a week, the Concord base was open and full of action. Cooking, packing, loading and delivering. It even got to a point where they were so inundated with orders that they had to set up a limit for what they could handle each day and evening.

Kawal's organisation skills came to the fore and in many ways were the calming influence everyone needed at a time when relationships were strained. At one point all three men of the family were at loggerheads as to how many hours a day each person needed to be at work. Each one thought the others weren't pulling their weight.

> "Kawal rounded them up and told them to shut up and be respectful. They obeyed her order because she very rarely raises her voice – but when she does, they all listen," Ash recalls.

This newly created take-away product also spawned another idea, which had more legs than just a stop-gap solution due to the COVID-19 pandemic.

It was called Manjits Home.

MANJITS AND THE TANDOOR OF SECRETS

The family's temporary model to get the business through tough times was about to be scaled up dramatically. Pitched to supermarkets, the selected dishes would be vacuum sealed and sent out to retailers with a shelf life of fourteen days.

Keeping it simple was the key. Nine well-known Indian dishes were decided on but not without some drama. Manjit wanted twenty-four dishes in the range, but Deep, the function centre chef, and Ash all protested reasoning that it was an opportunity to get into the market with an exclusive few, and then expand later.

In the end, that point-of-view prevailed, and nine dishes were included in the first Manjits Home range.

Delivering en masse, at high quality, was vital. In the backs of their minds was the worry of delivering a different type of taste to what a customer would receive at an event in the function centre or for a dinner at the restaurant.

The function centre chef made test batch after test batch to make sure this wouldn't upend the venture. Once he got the levels right, which took close to a week to master, it was full steam ahead.

How to price it was also a worry for Manjit and Deep. Would people be concerned that it was much cheaper to buy these in a supermarket than ordering it at a fine dining restaurant?

Portion size, and packaging with colourful, vibrant branding was a must. Ash wanted these packs to stand out from the crowd. Make people at least look, pick up, read and hopefully throw into their basket or trolley.

Deep had days of Zoom meetings with various retailers and selected service stations around Sydney and with good results. Many were keen and got on board early.

The first few weeks provided plenty of hiccups. The major headache was that people were complaining that the plastic which covered the tray melted into the food when heated in the oven. "Who knew there were different types of plastic for microwaves and oven use?" Deep looked into the problem and it was solved within a day. The next problem was the $20,000 mechanical machine used to apply the plastic wasn't coping with the constant use. A more expensive version was sorted and purchased before production continued.

Incredibly for Manjit it was a case of unfinished business. In the early 1990s, a deal with a multi-national food brand was on the boil.

In 1993, Manjit and his brother Surjeet started a company that made a deal with Birdseye for a similar product. However, before the deal could be finalised Birdseye was bought out by Dunlop, and the deal bit the dust. Money was lost as time and effort had already been put into sourcing ingredients, warehousing and transport options.

> "It could have been done to a very high scale, but things were not in favour," Manjit admitted. "The cash flow of the restaurants was suffering as the profits and energy were going into the commercial project instead. We had to stem the flow and go back to basics.
>
> "It was a plan which would have seen the business skyrocket and put the modest eateries onto a higher plane as it would have gone through the roof. My brother and I were scouting around Sydney to find warehouses that could hold the mass production. I believe that, had this gone ahead, we may not even have had restaurants right now. It would have taken over. It bugged me for years and gave me sleepless nights. Could I have done something better back then? Should I have done anything different? Would I ever get another chance like that again?"

Who knows what may have resulted? Manjit also admitted that, at the time, he was burning the candle at both ends and wasn't putting all his energies into the eateries, so everything started to suffer.

> "You can take your eye off the ball and although you can keep doing the job, if you sit back and take a look you can see the quality isn't there."

Funnily those words are similar to the reason Varun couldn't continue with the bowling club venture. Many entrepreneurs learn that keeping focused can be the key to success.

Nonetheless, Manjit's experience from twenty-five years beforehand became a valuable source of knowledge on how to navigate through the impending shutdown. He saw it as a second chance, an opportunity to make amends.

Manjit hadn't told his sons or Ash about the Birdseye deal until the new products hit the shelves. The boys wondered why their dad knew so much when it came to the various aspects of putting together the venture. They realised as soon as he told them. It was the perfect 'learn from your mistakes' type situation.

Deep says, that on more than one occasion, he has ducked into some of the supermarkets selling the range and stood near the refrigerated section where the packs were sold, just to see if people were actually buying them.

> *"I felt like a stalker. At one point someone recognised me and asked if Varun was chucking a sickie and I was picking up some meals to serve customers. The smart-arse."*

The success of this foray into the retail market has now opened up another shelf filler, but surprisingly not another Indian dish. Deep and Ash held discussions on venturing into doing the same as the Manjit seal packs but with Thai food. The fact that some Thai curries are similar to some Indian servings meant making a red or green curry wouldn't be too hard.

Indian curries typically contain turmeric and coriander but is not as heavy in the sauce as Thai curry. On the other hand, Thai versions use a variety of curry pastes, mixed with coconut milk.

Packaged as 'Siams', the road into another country's cuisine started with the release of just two dinners—Red Curry and Green Curry.

With the lifting of Covid restrictions and people slowly starting to dine out again, another headache has popped up—though this one is for better reasons. The production of the seal packs cannot continue in the function centre as weddings are back.

Finding a new home base to fulfil the requirements of the retail arm is now a necessity. Now the market is there, expanding that side of the business is the goal.

COVID-19 is still changing the world. Early in the piece, owning a business in many ways exposed the financial fragility of many. As the pandemic caused massive dislocation among small businesses, especially prior to the availability of government aid, only the strong survived without too much damage. Sadly, for many, it was an easier decision to shut up shop.

This family proved they had the business nous to get through to the other side. They could have let go of staff and sat it out until all was clear. But no, they continued to give a living to people, they faced it head on and won—while unexpectedly creating new ventures that will continue.

The family unit pulled together as one when it so vitally had to. Manjit, Deep, Varun, and Kawal's work ethic from years past stood them in good stead. Their mantra of the 'glass is half full, not half empty' served them well.

PART 3

Customers

Funny or mean, nice or not, friendly or critical, no business can survive without its customers. Anyone who has worked in customer service can tell you stories of the wildest customers, from the strange to the hilarious to the downright dangerous. For an establishment like Manjits, this goes tenfold. These are just some of the stories they have to share of the most memorable events over the years!

Nearly Taking One for the Team

It was a warm Saturday afternoon in 2007. Something was bothering twenty-five-year-old Deep as he walked along Concord's main street to the family-owned function centre.
With his parents overseas, he had been handed the baton to run the family business for the first time.

A wedding reception had been booked for that night for around 600 people. It should have been just another run-of-the-mill job, but the phrase 'expect the unexpected' was about to become reality.

Deep was already experienced in handling the company's functions and weddings, so he knew that, despite the best planning, it is not always possible to predict things that can happen out of the blue. But what was about to play out in the next few hours would top the list of anything he had ever seen, even to this day.

MANJITS AND THE TANDOOR OF SECRETS

A meeting in the function centre months earlier between Deep, the Turkish bride-to-be, and her Lebanese future husband had shown no signs of trouble. No alarm bells going off; no eyebrows raised. The pair were madly in love and haggled a price for the reception before putting down a healthy-sized deposit to set the date in stone. A strategy to place some guests away from others and avoid confrontation was spoken about, but Deep knew that was normal for most weddings.

He arrived at the centre and, as always, had a meeting with the event and kitchen staff to check on the run sheet and all the arrangements. He generally finished the meeting with a pep talk reminding staff that this was a big night for the families, but this time he also laid bare his concerns.

"Something isn't right. Stay on your toes for this one. I don't know what it is," he said.

Many of his staff looked at each other, smiling, thinking, it's just 'Deep being Deep'. Events come with challenges and the Gujrals have faced some big ones in the past.

Dealing adeptly with unexpected problems is Deep's forte and there is never a shortage of those throughout a function. Deep himself says a behind-the-scenes look might be reminiscent of a Fawlty Towers episode, with Deep doing his best to keep it all looking poised and calm on the surface before a situation spirals out of control and into a disastrous mess.

As the guests started to arrive for the Turkish-Lebanese reception, the canapes and drinks came out on cue. But even before the bubbles in the champagne flutes could disappear, Deep could see the room was fractured.

You could have drawn a line right down the middle with a five-metre buffer zone on either side.

It's a situation more common than many realise, but those rough seas can be navigated by an experienced crew of staff, and the company's 'A-team' were already onto it. Keeping service regular over shorter periods is usually one of the better distraction plans, but this was a tough crowd.

MANJITS AND THE TANDOOR OF SECRETS

Deep was starting to become more wary as the room grew tenser by the minute. He turned to his second in charge and said, "We haven't even got this mob seated yet and it feels like the lead-up to the war scene in Braveheart."

He could hear stones hitting glass, assuming it was children taking expensive white pebbles out of pot plant bases in the foyer, and fire them at one another in a pretend battle.

Little did they know that a real 'adult battle' was brewing in the ladies' powder room. It was one of the women complaining to a friend stating loudly that the parents of the children should be brought into line.

Another woman angrily flung open a cubicle door and shouted, "How dare you say that—say it to my face, you bitch."

At that, it was on for young and old in the ladies' powder room. A physical altercation was underway. Hair pulling, slaps, and then punches flew. More women became involved, causing a ripple effect which saw more people—women and men—rushing to the powder room to join in the chaos, with the warring parties spilling over into the foyer of the building.

Within seconds, the foyer was reminiscent of a saloon bar brawl in the wild west. Chairs were being thrown, glasses smashed, clothes ripped, people fainting on the floor.

In shock and wondering how the situation could be any worse, Deep only had to turn his head to see it was a serious as it gets, because he found himself staring at a pistol.

In the north of India, celebratory firing of guns is a feature at weddings in rural towns that in some cases can lead to a fatality by accident.

But make no mistake. This dude wasn't from the northern provinces of India wanting to replicate shooting to the sky. This was a huge, angry and agitated man who clearly wasn't thinking straight.

Deep remembers it vividly.

"I'm brown-skinned. For the first time in my life, I believe I turned white. I could feel the beads of sweat forming on my forehead. I'm told the whole room stopped fighting and instead turned their attention to the gunman and me.

"This guy had his shirt off and looked like the size of a heavyweight cage fighter. All I could say was 'please put the gun down, so we can all go in and pretend this didn't happen. I'm sure we can sort this out and no one gets hurt'.

"In hindsight that was probably a pretty stupid thing to say. As if we'd go in and carry on like nothing happened. It's a wonder he didn't shoot me just for saying that. I continued by saying, 'no one has called the police, just leave. Go.' To my amazement, he did just that."

The gunman's hand started to fidget, either with nerves or realising the intensity of the moment. The crowd which had formed a ring around the pair fell silent. His eyes glassy, lips quivering, the gunman raced out the door into the night, and was never seen again.

Deep dodged a bullet that night. Literally.

The incident created attention on all Sydney news bulletins the next day. The close call even spread back to India and more importantly his father, Manjit and mother, Kawal.

His mum screamed down the phone, "Are you okay, my boy? I don't know what I would have done if you died."

His dad, never one to be too emotional at the best of times asked, "Was there any food wasted?"

Deep replied, "The food survived, Dad. And so did I. Thanks for asking."

Celebs

Chandigarh, India in the 1960s and 1970s saw modernisation, industrialisation and westernisation come to the fore, underpinning economic and social development that began under Prime Minister Jawaharlal Nehru.

Manjit Gujral grew up in a Sikh household that saw multiple families living under one roof. His father, Makhan, worked as a senior director of an insurance company, while his mother, Manmohan, was employed as a house caretaker. With his two brothers, three sisters, and plenty of cousins in the same household, there was always plenty going on.

It was a strict Sikh upbringing where education was held in high esteem. The extended family system meant Manjit didn't even know who his own father was until later in life. The reason for that is the entire responsibility for maintenance of the household and social relations falls upon the father and no one can question his authority. So, with multiple dads living under the one roof calling the shots, infant minds have trouble working out which one to call 'Papa'.

Many days were spent playing and watching cricket with neighbourhood kids on red dirt until the sun went down. To this day, India's love for the game has thousands of kids rolling their arms over attempting to master the perfect Anil Kumble leg break or mimicking a Virat Kohli-like cover drive as they dare to dream.

MANJITS AND THE TANDOOR OF SECRETS

Manjit was a kid with no grand sporting plans. He was, however, good friends with someone who would be regarded as one of the greatest all-rounders to ever play the game.

Kapil Dev has godlike status in India and the Gujral's had front-row seats to the making of a champion and a legend.

The future national skipper would play for hours even on the hottest days, making his mistakes and importantly, learning from them as his technique become his cornerstone to future triumphs, both personally and for his country. Manjit recalls:

"I remember he was a good cricketer with potential - but there were many at the time who promised so much. It wasn't until his teenage years he started to stand out from the pack. Interestingly he never forgot or left behind his friends as his fame and fortune took off on an international stage. He often came to the restaurant when on tour here, which would coincide with his birthday. We've held some great parties for Kapil."

Dev is just one of the many celebrities from all realms to visit Manjit's restaurant when in town and although having star-power doesn't necessarily make or break the success of an establishment, it certainly doesn't hurt.

Politicians, star musicians, radio shock jocks and sporting celebrities are just some of the mix that regularly pop-in for long lunches and dinners and have done so since the beginning in Potts Point.

When they were still at their first restaurant in Potts Point, the 'Two Ronnies' were doing a shoot in Australia and wanted some Indian cuisine after a long day filming.

A short man with an English accent walked in. "Can I get a table for two? Your food is so good. I was in here yesterday to pick up a takeaway," said Ronnie Corbett.

Not knowing who he was, Manjit replied. "Yes, but you'll have to wait your turn, just like everyone else. We're busy."

Corbett took the advice, turned and walked out and stood with his mate Ronnie Barker on the Potts Point footpath until a table became available.

When Manjit found out later that night, that the pair were in fact two of the biggest names of British comedy, Manjit apologised and asked if a picture could be taken with them. Corbett replied, "You'll have to wait, we're busy."

Silence. Then laughter all-round as Manjit wiped the sweat off his brow.

In 2019, Ash Reynolds was given the task of giving the cosy setting in Balmain a makeover. It was long overdue, but he also knew it wouldn't be easy. Getting Manjit's tick of approval would be the hardest part and Ash admits that, in hindsight, a little more consultation throughout the process may have been beneficial.

"Taking down the pictures of the celebs was a big mistake," Ash groans, as he put his hands to his forehead. "I was just after a more modern take on the place. I now know it was a bit like taking the medals of a war veteran and putting them in a draw. Having proof that famous people had dined there was a crowning glory, so to speak."

After weeks of renovations, the major overhaul produced a vastly different look to its previous form. The walls were changed to a dark charcoal to highlight the artwork painted personally by Kawal. A towering painting of Annapurna, Hindu goddess of food and nourishment, was a showstopper overlooking the dining balcony.

The day had come to show Manjit. All the new colours, table placements, sketched drawings were not even looked at. Manjit knew the pictures wouldn't be there and he was totally focused on the ensuing argument to make sure they were put back in their rightful place.

By that afternoon they were.

When it comes to catering for the rich and famous, the modern version in Darling Harbour is quickly catching up.

The lavish interior, drenched in glass is located on the water in the trendy locale of Barangaroo in Sydney. It cost close to one million dollars to renovate when they bought it in 2018 and it is now the flagship facility. It is a far cry from the humble beginnings of their first restaurant at Potts Point and their later Balmain digs.

Arnold Schwarzenegger's visit turned plenty of heads as diners looked in amazement, some shaking their heads in disbelief that they were in the same room as the movie star and former Republican Governor of California.

The moment Schwarzenegger walked through the doors it was as if time stood still and everything went into slow motion.

Even the best waiters who were rostered on especially for the visit were feeling starstruck and in awe by a man who is recognised around the world. Schwarzenegger wore an Armani suit, which looked two sizes too big, a t-shirt that didn't match, and a pair of joggers. Both Deep and Varun—who dress to impress—were surprised.

The night went off without a hitch. 'The Terminator' demolished the menu's signature dish and a Naan bread the size of a garbage lid and thanked his hosts with his signature saying, "I'll be back."

Not all heavy hitters are that easy to please. Walking on eggshells sometimes is needed as demands can come thick and fast from people who are used to being waited on hand and foot.

India's highest political figure is one person you don't want to get on the wrong side of. President Ram Nath Kovind of India came to Australia in 2018 to help strengthen the relationship between the two countries. After meeting with the then Prime Minister Scott Morrison and the former Governor-General Peter Cosgrove early in the day, and unveiling a Mahatma Gandhi statue in Parramatta, the President planned to finish the day at Manjits for a private reception.

With his wife Savita by his side, the President strode into the restaurant smiling and looking majestic, with an entourage large enough for a pop superstar to be proud of.

However, what should have been a moment to savour for the family turned into a thirty-six-hour ordeal.

"He came here and looked down at everyone. He thought I was the waiter and constantly clicked his fingers at me when he wanted something. I had to just suck it up the whole time," explains Deep. He recounts a story etched in his memory.

The president wanted a Guava juice. Deep brought him one with ice but he proclaimed that he didn't want ice. The juice was taken back, a new one prepared without ice, but then the President declared that it wasn't cold enough.

Varun isn't someone to get flustered easily but he knew this was a night where, if he was off his game, it would haunt him for the rest of his days. News travels fast, especially if you're an Indian chef, and the thought of getting bad press from what would normally be a routine meal, made the man with the apron nervous.

"I wasn't aware of just how big the night was going to be," Varun says. "It was like something out of a movie. The entourage was also demanding and nothing about the night was as straight forward as what we first thought it would be. It wasn't an ordinary night at the office."

Unfortunately for Deep, the night didn't stop when the Presidential entourage left.

After closing up late that night, hitting the pillow couldn't come quick enough for the few that endured the tough shift.

Then a 'phone call.

It was the advisor for the President. "The President would like some Tandoori vegetables delivered to his hotel suite."

"Mate, we're closed. The kitchen is shut and everyone has gone home," Deep responded.

MANJITS AND THE TANDOOR OF SECRETS

"Listen, the President is hungry. Could you please get him what he wants? My job is on the line," was the reply.

Eight phone calls later to find a staff member willing to come back to work, and a drive to the restaurant to open up, President Kovind got his Tandoori vegetables.

Some Like It Hot

A young couple walked through the doors of the Balmain restaurant on a warm Sydney evening.

The man wore a blue pin-striped suit with a white crisp shirt, unbuttoned at the top and shiny black, pointy shoes that Fred Astaire would be proud of. On his arm, a beautiful, curvaceous woman in a short black dress that sparkled as she walked, while her red high heels caught the carpet on every second step.

Their arrival was show-stopping. The rest of the diners stared and thought they must be famous types who regularly visit the establishment. But no, this was just a first date. The two were obviously keen to impress by appearance and it certainly worked on the full house of diners.

The waiter seated the pair by the window as they were given a wine list. Both hardly spoke, apart from one-word pleasantries and stating their names were Kenji and Dianne. After ordering a bottle of Hunter Valley Verdelho, Kenji gave back the food menu and asked if he could get the hottest curry available. His date played it safe, ordering the Butter Chicken.

Varun's eyebrows raised when the ticket came across the food bench. 'Hottest curry' it read.

MANJITS AND THE TANDOOR OF SECRETS

The fact Kenji was from Japan made Varun send out a basic Vindaloo, which is hot, thinking that Wasabi heat isn't like chilli heat. *He'd handle it*, he thought.

One bite and Kenji screws up his face and quickly waves to the waiter. "This is nowhere near hot enough. I want it hotter please," he says.

The staff member comes back with a half-smile on her face as she knows Varun will now give it a real kick. More chilli is added, fresh Thai green and red powder. *A decent whack*, Varun thought.

The waitress serves again but waits on this occasion to get Kenji's tick of approval. A healthy size mouthful goes down his mouth, seconds later his eyes start to roll. Again, he says, "Not hot enough, I want it hotter." And adds, "I thought Indians loved their hot stuff."

There is the perception that Indians do love hot food. The hotter the better some think. There are many that do enjoy a 'hit of heat', but most would rather experience flavour instead.

Back to date night, and Kenji was talking perfectly despite the two chilli blasts. It was amazing to the staff as they knew that not many ask for a third top-up.

Varun thought to himself, *this man is trying to impress this woman, that's the reason he's doing this. He must be feeling like pulling the flowers out of the vase and downing the water from it but he's being 'Mr Cool'.*

"I'll fix him up now," he said.

Kawal interjected. "You can't send it out hotter. It'll kill him," she said with a worried look on her face.

"It's OK, Mum. This time I'm just throwing in a bit more chilli as well as some chilli extract—it'll be fine."

MANJITS AND THE TANDOOR OF SECRETS

But again the plate comes back. It's still not hot enough.

"Jesus, who is this guy?" Varun yelled. "Is he actually eating this? Or is he pretending to?"

"He is," the waitress replied.

"F... this, he's in for it now," says Varun.

It was time the big guns were called in.

Varun had previously made a heat sensation which some say can make you feel like you're on the verge of a heart attack. It's called 'the ghost', a chilli flavour so ferocious it leaves you 'white as a ghost' once consumed.

Varun rarely pulls this out of his repertoire unless it is specifically asked for. It uses chilli extract for the base instead of chilli oil, which instantly has an effect. The kitchen staff were in tears almost as soon as it touched the pan. Coughing fits started for some as others cried in pain. This was an experienced Indian kitchen crew. Kawal had to leave. It was really a case of 'if you can't stand the heat, get out of the kitchen' kind of moment. Varun tasted it and his mouth was on fire.

The dish was sent out with more chilli than curry in it. If Kenji didn't like this, then Varun was going to give up, defeated.

A dozen eyes were staring out of every portal of the kitchen, waiting for the moment.

A small cheer went up as the sight of Kenji eating the serving was a culinary delight of a different kind. Beads of sweat are falling from his hair. His white shirt starts to become see-through. At this point, he's halfway through the dish and Varun sends a beer out on the house because in his words, "shit, this is impressive."

But then, it all turned nasty. A visceral scream that diners had never heard from a human before fills the restaurant as Kenji jumps out of his chair. Dianne is in shock as Kenji starts to run around the restaurant floor like a headless chook.

This had become the date from hell.

At one point Kenji started looking for glasses of water to down on fellow diner's tables. If there had been flowers in vases on tables, it's a fair bet he would have tipped the flower water down his neck too.

The pain was unbearable, Kenji collapsed on the carpet as everyone rushed to help.

"Call an ambulance now," yelled a diner.

Within minutes an ambulance arrived and soon Kenji and his date were quickly ushered into the back of the van by paramedics and taken to hospital.

After being told of the incident, Deep came into the restaurant the next day demanding answers as to what happened and why a customer had been given the super-charged food in the first place.

"I don't care if the bloody customer wants to burn their arse off. We can't appease them to the point of nearly killing them," he shouted at his brother.

Varun argued that Kenji asked for it and even wheeled out the line, 'the customer is always right.'

That didn't wash with Deep who prides the business on getting the job done with no risk involved.

Kenji came out of hospital hours later with a rasping sore throat and a big dose of embarrassment but admits he was showing off to impress his date. Kenji and Diane were married one year later and are now good friends with Varun. All can laugh about the incident.

Even though Varun rarely takes his big brother's advice, on this occasion he could understand where he was coming from. In saying that, he was never going to give his brother the satisfaction of knowing.

Manjit has seen plenty of people try and take on the heat test and shakes his head. He asks, why would someone risk spoiling a great night of dining?

Epilogue

Almost everyone knows of
a hard-working migrant family that owns
a food business. The ones that
make it their life to keep the doors open
and even have their kids working
from a young age.

Almost everyone knows of a hard-working migrant family that owns a food business. The ones that make it their life to keep the doors open and even have their kids working from a young age.

In my suburb in Newcastle, Australia, there was a fish and chip shop owned by a Greek family with three sons who all shared chores. From peeling and cutting spuds for chips, to making milkshakes or even mopping floors. No one shirked responsibility. Their work ethic rubbed off on the boys who became successful business owners in their own right.

The Gujrals are similar.

MANJITS AND THE TANDOOR OF SECRETS

Not settling for just turning over a tidy profit, this group looks to push boundaries. Nothing stands in their way, as the family dares to dream.

Even COVID-19 produced a different way of doing things at a time when the food industry was on its knees, which even surprised themselves.

The dynamics of any family can cause tension. The one thing that overrides everything when things get heated in this family unit is love. They squabble, they bitch, they overreact but by the next day, it's a clean slate.

The Gujral men fight like cat and dog but it's more like a debate. Who can beat each other in a contest? It never comes to blows or continuing slanging matches. And if it does, Kawal soothes the savage beasts with quiet understanding as she tiptoes through the carnage in a bid not to upset any of the three warring parties.

Manjit, now in his 70s, and Kawal both have every reason to put their feet up and rest.

Years of hard work serving thousands of dishes has never seemed to have taken a toll though. The busier it gets, the more they thrive. You get a sense they still enjoy every second of an honest day's work.

One thing I learned most in writing this was about the complexity of Indian culture.

Maybe I was simply ignorant before, but I've met a lot of people from India who were never like this family. Some I've met have been rude to the point where I probably tarred them all with the same brush.

Was that being racist? Yes, probably. Do I feel bad about that now? Yes, I do.

Manjit and Kawal do not see themselves as trailblazers. They know how difficult those early days were almost 40 years ago. They struggled at times, but they made it through and continue to strive to be the best people they can.

The high-pressure business of running wedding functions and ceremonies is one that many would bypass in an instant. This family takes every gig and navigates through the turmoil, like a badge of honour.

Manjits is a successful business story, but it is also a migrant story. One with all the highs and lows, and challenges, opportunities, and setbacks that many encounter, as well as what happens when the second generation wants to start doing things their own way.

I hope this book has given you a laugh, led you to have a think, and you have taken something away from these pages.

I hope it helps open your mind to how challenging life can get for those landing on our shores.

Amongst those we welcome in future, there is bound to more Manjits stories in the making.

Recipes from the Gujrals

ALL OUR RECIPES SERVE 4

SOMETHING MY PARENTS MADE

Palak Paneer

A RECIPE FROM MANJIT

The beautiful Green Fields of Punjab are famous for their spinach and mustard. I remember as a young boy growing up and playing along with my friends in the fields my parents would always call and ask our neighbours to find the kids to bring them home. There's nothing more quintessential than Palak Paneer in any Indian household. It is the lifeblood of the Punjab household and spinach takes the lead as the staple amongst the vegetarian dishes. Apart from being so simple to make, it is rifled with flavour—exactly what you need after a long day playing in the fields.

MANJITS AND THE TANDOOR OF SECRETS

Palak Paneer

INGREDIENTS

3 tablespoons	Manjits Masala Curry Sauce
400g	Fresh English spinach
2 tablespoons	Vegetable oil
1 teaspoon	Cumin seeds
1 tablespoon	Garam masala
4	Tomatoes, diced
500g	Paneer cheese cubes
100g	Freshly grated ginger
2 tablespoons	Mustard seed oil
1½ tablespoons	Chopped fresh coriander
2-3	Garlic cloves, crushed
1	Chopped green chilli

SOMETHING MY PARENTS MADE

METHOD

1. Put the English spinach in a colander or large bowl. Pour over boiling hot water to wilt the leaves. Drain the water and then add cold water. Drain well once again and purée in a food processor or blender.
2. Heat the vegetable oil for deep frying in a heavy-based pan to 190°C. Deep fry the paneer for 2-3 minutes, until the paneer starts to golden brown on the sides.
Set aside on kitchen paper to drain.
DO NOT OVER FRY the paneer.
3. In another separate saucepan, heat 2-3 tablespoons of the mustard oil over a medium heat and add the cumin seeds. You will notice that they crackle. Following that, add the chopped tomatoes, ginger, garlic, green chilli and Manjits paste and cook for 5-7 minutes.
4. Add the wilted spinach and stir. Bring this mixture to a simmer, then mix in the paneer cubes.
5. Put in a serving dish and sprinkle with the garam masala and coriander.
6. Garnish by crushing 1 paneer cube on top of the final preparation.
7. Enjoy with steaming hot Indian chickpea flatbread... i.e. missi roti!

SOMETHING MY PARENTS MADE

Mixed Vegetable Jalfrezi

A RECIPE FROM KAWAL

Growing up in Rajasthan (a predominantly vegetarian state) I was blessed to be surrounded by wonderful fresh vegetables. Unlike today's vegetables you buy at the markets they had a unique 'non-preservative' sort of flavour to them. They were truly organic.

MANJITS AND THE TANDOOR OF SECRETS

Mixed Vegetable Jalfrezi

INGREDIENTS

FOR KADAI MASALA POWDER

2 tablespoons	Coriander seeds
1 tablespoon	Cumin
½ tablespoon	Poppy seeds
1-2 pods	Green cardamom
2 medium size	Kashmiri red chillies

FOR CURRY

½ cup (chopped)	Potato
½ cup (chopped)	Carrot
½ cup (chopped)	Beans
¼ cup (fresh)	Green peas
12 florets	Cauliflower
½ cup (chopped)	Capsicum
2 tablespoons	Ghee
1 or 2	Bay leaf
2 (finely chopped)	Onion
1 tablespoon	Ginger garlic crushed
1 teaspoon	Turmeric powder
2 tablespoons	Red chilli powder
1 cup	Tomato puree
1 tablespoon	Fenugreek seeds (also known as kasuri methi)
¼ tablespoon	Garam masala powder
A few (finely chopped)	Coriander leaves
2 tablespoons	Cooking oil
As needed	Salt

SOMETHING MY PARENTS MADE

METHOD

MAKING THE KADAI MASALA

1. Take a mid-sized pan and whack it on a low flame.
2. When the pan is hot enough, add 2 teaspoons of coriander seeds, 1 teaspoon of cumin seeds, ½ teaspoon of poppy seeds, 2 Kashmiri red chillies and 1 green cardamom and roast them until aromatic - this will take about 3 minutes.
3. Once cool, grind spices in a mortar and pestle then keep aside.

MAKING THE DISH

4. Take a large frypan and add 2 tablespoons of cooking oil (or better yet mustard oil) and place on a low flame.
5. When the cooking oil is hot enough, add ½ cup of chopped potato, ½ cup of chopped carrot, and ½ cup of chopped beans and sauté them for about 2 minutes.
6. Then add ¼ cup of fresh green peas, 12 small cauliflower florets, ½ cup chopped capsicum and a little bit of salt, sauté them for about 3 to 4 minutes until there is a little color change.
7. Transfer them all into a plate and keep them aside.
8. In the same frypan, add 2 teaspoons of ghee along with a bay leaf and 2 onions which have been finely chopped and a teaspoon of ginger garlic crushed then sauté them well for about 7-8 minutes.
9. Add turmeric powder, red chilli powder and mix them well for 3 minutes.
10. Add 1 cup of tomato puree and mix in for about 2 minutes.
11. Add fenugreek seeds, ¼ teaspoon of garam masala powder and the prepared kadai masala powder.
12. Add some water as required to adjust gravy consistency then cook on a low flame until the cooking oil separates.
13. Add in the sautéed veggies and mix them well.
14. Cover the saucepan and cook it for about 3 to 4 minutes on a low flame.
15. Add a few coriander leaves which have been finely chopped and salt and pepper to taste.

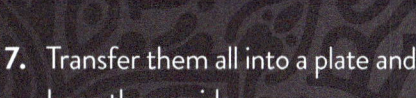

SOMETHING THE GRANDKIDS LOVE

Vegetable Samosa

A RECIPE FROM KAWAL

My granddaughter Nishka was obsessed with samosas when she first had them. She went through this phase of wanting them at every meal and would polish them off in minutes. My grandson, Ziv, on the other hand, loves the crispy pastry on the outside but sits there pulling out every pea he sees inside. For the adults this is the ultimate comfort food and perfect on cold rainy days.

MANJITS AND THE TANDOOR OF SECRETS

Vegetable Samosa

INGREDIENTS

FOR THE PASTRY

1 cup	Refined white flour
1 cup	Ghee (Pepe Saya makes a good one)
½ teaspoon	Carom seeds (or 'ajwain') (this is optional)
2 tablespoons	Vegetable oil
A pinch of	Salt

FOR THE STUFFING

4 medium	Potatoes cut into small cubes
½ cup	Frozen green peas (1 cup if you're Nishka!)
2 tablespoons	Vegetable Oil
1 teaspoon	Cumin seeds
2-3cm	Ginger peeled and chopped
2 small	Green chillies chopped
1 teaspoon	Red chilli powder
Salt	To taste
1 teaspoon	Dry mango powder (Indians call it amchur)
1 teaspoon	Garam masala powder
1 teaspoon	Fresh coriander leaves chopped
1 tablespoon	Manjits Masala Curry Paste

METHOD

FOR THE PASTRY

1. Mix the pastry ingredients. Add water slowly and make a hard dough. Keep it under a wet cloth for 10 to 15 minutes - it will slightly soften.
2. Meanwhile cook green peas in salted boiling water till soft. Refresh in cold water so they become firm.

MAKING THE FILLING

3. Heat oil in a pan, add the cumin seeds and you'll notice that they start to change colour.
4. Add ginger and cook though for 5 minutes.
5. Add green chillies and cook 1 minute.
6. Then add and potatoes, red chilli powder, salt, amchur, and garam masala powder. Cook for 2 minutes.
7. Add in the Manjits curry masala paste and cook till the colour comes through the mixture. Should be a nice yellowy-orange.
8. Stir the preparation really well. Your home will smell amazing.
9. Sprinkle a dash of water and cook covered till potatoes are nice and soft. Add the green peas to the mixture.

BRINGING IT TOGETHER

10. Divide up the dough into about twenty equal portions and roll them into balls. Hint: oil your hands slightly so it doesn't stick to your hands.
11. Apply a little flour and roll them into four inch diameter elongated 'disks' - you can use a rolling pin for this. Then, cut into halfs, apply water on the edges.
12. Shape into a cone and stuff it with the potato and peas filling that you made earlier.
13. Seal the edges with your fingertips well and deep fry in medium hot oil till crisp and golden brown.
14. Drain onto an absorbent paper towel or baking paper to take out the excess oil.
15. Serve hot with mint or tamarind chutney and watch out for little fingers... they are usually the first to grab them!

THE FAMILY HEIRLOOM

Butter Chicken

THE TRADITIONAL WAY

There is no difference in taste between the two Butter Chicken dishes. The difference comes in the preparation and, importantly, the presentation as you can see from the two photographs. On the facing page is The Traditional Way as created by the Gujral's ancestor Kundal Lal and beloved by Manjit. On page 84, you will see The Modern Spin which Varun has developed. Regardless of which option you choose to cook, both are full of flavour and guaranteed to be enjoyed!

MANJITS AND THE TANDOOR OF SECRETS

Butter Chicken

INGREDIENTS

TO MARINATE THE CHICKEN

600 grams	Boneless chicken fillets
2 tablespoons	Thick yogurt (or Greek yogurt - see notes)
1 teaspoon	Coriander powder
2 teaspoons	Kashmiri red chilli powder
2 teaspoons	Ginger-garlic paste
1 teaspoon	Garam masala powder
2 tablespoons	Lime
1 teaspoon	Salt

TO MAKE THE GRAVY

½ cup	Cashew nuts
1 cup	Chopped tomatoes
2-3	Whole green cardamoms
3-4	Whole black peppercorns
2-3cm	Cinnamon stick
3-4	Cloves
3 tablespoons	Butter (salted or unsalted)
2	Whole black cardamoms
2 teaspoons	Kashmiri red chilli powder
½ cup	Onions, chopped
2 tablespoons	Tomato paste
50 grams	Khoya (crumbled) - see notes
½ cup	Full cream
2 teaspoons	Fenugreek seeds
1 tablespoon	Lime juice

THE FAMILY HEIRLOOM

METHOD

MARINATE THE CHICKEN

1. Wash the chicken fillets and drain any extra water. Cut the chicken into approximately 4cm cubes. Remember they will shrink 20% when cooking.
2. In a stainless steel or glass bowl mix the chicken pieces with the thick yogurt, coriander powder, Kashmiri red chilli powder, ginger-garlic paste, garam masala powder, lime juice, and add a touch of salt.
3. Cover the bowl and throw it into the fridge. Let the chicken marinate for 2-3 hours or better yet… overnight! The longer the chicken marinates, the softer and juicier it will become.

COOK THE CHICKEN

4. Preheat the oven to 200°C.
5. Arrange the nicely marinated chicken on a baking sheet lined with aluminium foil. Lining the tray with foil makes the clean-up super easy at the end.
6. Roast for about 30 minutes, until the chicken is nicely browned and tender. It's best if you can get the pieces a bit burned at the edges while keeping the rest of the chicken slightly undercooked.

VARUN'S HINT
You can broil the chicken for 5 minutes to get that charred colour and flavour

MANJIT'S HINT
You can also grill the marinated chicken in a skillet over the BBQ

MANJITS AND THE TANDOOR OF SECRETS

MAKE THE GRAVY

7. Heat 4 cups of water in a pan over medium-high heat.
8. When it comes to the boil, add cashew nuts, tomatoes, onions, whole green cardamoms, whole black cardamoms, cinnamon stick, cloves, and whole black peppercorns to the water.
9. Cook for about 8 to 10 minutes on a medium heat.
10. Drain the water and add the boiled ingredients to a blender along with ½ cup of water. Blend to make a nice smooth paste. Pass the paste through a fine-mesh strainer and try to keep pressing the paste with the back of a spoon to get maximum smooth paste. Discard the rough residue.

METHOD

1. Heat butter in a pan over medium-high heat.
2. Once the butter is melted, add in the Kashmiri red chilli powder and sauté for about 2-3 seconds. Adding red chilli powder to hot butter gives a lovely colour to the curry.
3. Be quick after adding the red chilli powder otherwise it may burn.
4. Add the cashew nut paste to the pan along with ½ cup water and cook for about 4-5 minutes.
5. Now add salt, tomato paste, khoya, processed cheese, full cream, fenugreek, and lime juice to the pan and cook for 2-3 minutes.
6. Remove the chicken from the oven and add it to the pan (chicken can be made even 1 day prior). Adjust the gravy by adding more water if needed. Check for salt and cook for a further 2-3 minutes.
7. Garnish with swirls of cream, fresh coriander leaves and serve super-hot. Perfect with Garlic Naan.

THE FAMILY HEIRLOOM

To make thick yogurt, add some plain yogurt to a fine-mesh strainer and let the strainer sit over a bowl for an hour. The liquid from the yogurt will drip down in the bowl and you will be left with thick yogurt in the strainer. You can also use Greek yogurt in place of thick yogurt (much easier).

If khoya is not available, mix ¼ cup dry milk powder with some milk and make a dough. Use it in place of khoya.

THE FAMILY HEIRLOOM

Butter Chicken

THE MODERN SPIN

WHEN MARINATING THE CHICKEN

1. Try to get the WHOLE chicken breasts 'Kyiv-style' on the bone (about 220gms each). This will allow the meat to stay juicy and moist. Do not cut or slice the chicken into cubes. The rest of the marination is exactly the same.
2. Place a couple of diagonal 1cm deep slits into the chicken. It allows the marination to penetrate into the meat.

WHEN GRILLING THE CHICKEN

3. Set the temperature of the oven to a lower setting than the traditional version. This will allow for the meat to cook internally for a slightly longer period of time (say 175°). Because we are using a larger chunk of meat, we need the meat to cook right through. (about 30 minutes).
4. This modern version is best cooked in the oven as it allows for a good circulation of the marination on the meat and helps the marinade to stick together. Do not use the barbecue or skillet for this.

WHEN MAKING THE GRAVY

5. Although making the gravy is relatively the same we do recommend adding a few stems of coriander and leaves of coriander into the mix. It will give a nice refreshing citrus flavour to the sauce when blending it.
6. Add a few whole cashew nuts and a dollop of honey into the sauce.
7. Once the chicken and sauce is cooked pour the hot sauce over the chicken breast.
8. This time garnish with crushed cashew nuts sprinkled on top and some fresh green chilli and finely diced tomato.
9. This "modern version" is best had with Kashmiri Pilau rice and enjoyed with a fork and knife rather than a spoon!

OUR BEST SELLER

Tandoori Chicken

A RECIPE FROM VARUN

Nearly every ethnicity has a preparation involving chicken which is often favoured by people with palates that prefer plainer food. The Japanese have Karaage, the Portuguese Peri-Peri, there is the Middle Eastern Shish Kebab, Chinese Honey Chicken, or the American delicacy of KFC! Tandoori Chicken is the Indian contribution. Its tender, flavoursome, and not going to destroy anyone's taste buds – a 'safe bet' that many look for on a menu!

MANJITS AND THE TANDOOR OF SECRETS

Tandoori Chicken

INGREDIENTS

1	Whole chicken, skinned and cut
10	Cloves of garlic made into a paste
1	Onion grated
1 inch piece	Ginger made into a paste
½ cup	Greek yoghurt (labne can also be used)
2 tablespoons	White wine vinegar
5 tablespoons	Chilli powder
5 tablespoons	Smoky paprika
5 tablespoons	Ground red chilli
1 tablespoon	Chaat masala
½ teaspoon	Coriander powder
1 teaspoon	Cumin seeds powder
1½ teaspoons	Salt
1 teaspoon	Garam masala
1 teaspoon	Ghee
Juice	of 2 lemons
Zest	of lemon

OUR BEST SELLER

METHOD

1. Add the onion paste, garlic and ginger with the yoghurt.
2. Add in the spices to the yoghurt and mix thoroughly including lemon juice and zest.
3. Once the marinade is made marinate the chicken (use your hands - it will be easier).
4. Marinate for a minimum of 24 hours, but 48 hours is preferred, changing sides every 12 hours.
5. Once marinated, cook over charcoal so the flames lick the chicken and the oils enhance the smokey flavour.
6. Finish with a coating of ghee and Chatt masala.

SOMETHING INDIANS ALWAYS ORDER

Classic Kadai Chicken

A RECIPE FROM DEEP

Whenever I'm sitting with clients, they want something "different" in their events. Different decor, different colour schemes, new venues, everything has to be different... except the chicken curry. They always ask for the same classic chicken curry. There is no point even offering a different dish; we always take the scenic route and end up in the same location. Chicken Kadai is usually a dry chicken curry. However, in my family, we prefer to have a bit of gravy, which is why I add yoghurt. Just enough to create a thick gravy that can be eaten with roti or spooned over rice.

MANJITS AND THE TANDOOR OF SECRETS

Classic Kadai Chicken

INGREDIENTS

4-6 tablespoons	Mustard oil
1 whole	Chicken (bone-in skinless) cut into pieces
1 medium	Red onion diced
3 tablespoons	Manjits Masala Curry Sauce
½ cup	Greek yoghurt (optional)
1 tablespoon	Ginger-garlic paste
6-8 medium	Roma tomatoes chopped into small pieces
Salt	To taste
1 tablespoon	Lemon juice
1 tablespoon	Tomato paste
1 bunch	Coriander chopped
4-6	Green chillies sliced
½ teaspoon	Garam masala
½ teaspoon	Coriander seeds
½ teaspoon	Turmeric
½ teaspoon	Red chilli powder

SOMETHING INDIANS ALWAYS ORDER

METHOD

1. Heat 1 tablespoon oil, and fry onions till translucent and slightly golden on the edges, then add ginger and garlic and cook for a further 5 minutes.
2. Add tomatoes. Cook the tomatoes till they are soft, mashing them with a wooden spoon every few minutes.
3. Add the Manjits Curry Masala Sauce.
4. Add all the spices (Garam masala, Coriander seeds, Turmeric powder, Red chilli powder and the salt).
5. Add the chicken and the tomato paste.
6. Cook for 10 minutes, till the chicken colour changes from pink to white. With the lid on the cooker.
7. Add yoghurt (if using), turn heat to low and let it cook till the chicken is tender and cooked through. In case the chicken is sticking to the bottom, add a splash of water.
8. Add lemon juice.
9. Once the chicken is cooked through, add chopped green chillies, and chopped coriander.
10. Serve hot with naan or the next curry along the buffet.

SOMETHING NON-INDIANS ALWAYS ORDER

South Indian Fish Curry

A RECIPE FROM DEEP

I always have clients asking me for something that's seafood and mild. South Indian cuisine has a reputation of being too spicy, but this dish dispels that myth. What I find really interesting is that even people from the north of India are into the fish curry that we prepare! One day I was doing an event for an Australian friend of mine and decided to put some of this curry in the event, and to see the result. I was quite surprised to see how many people just absolutely smashed the curry. Since then, I have always recommended it to some of the events that we do that are not Indian.

MANJITS AND THE TANDOOR OF SECRETS

South Indian Fish Curry

INGREDIENTS

A swig	Olive oil
3 tablespoons	Manjits Curry Masala Sauce
2½ tablespoons	Grated ginger
2½	Garlic cloves, crushed
1 tablespoon	Black mustard seeds
12	Curry leaves
2	Brown onions, finely sliced
2 tablespoons	Turmeric powder
1½ tablespoons	Coriander powder
1½ tablespoons	Cumin powder
A pinch	Chilli flakes
1	Red chilli, chopped
450g	Vine ripened tomatoes, chopped
280ml pack	Coconut cream
1	Lime juiced
400-500g	Skinless firm white fish fillet, cut into 5cm fillet chunks
	Fresh coriander leaves to garnish
	Extra lime wedges to serve
	Steamed basmati rice to serve

SOMETHING NON-INDIANS ALWAYS ORDER

METHOD

1. Heat the oil in a large frying pan or sauté pan with a lid and fry the mustard seeds and curry leaves until they start to pop and smell fragrant.
2. Stir in the onion until translucent and edges golden up.
3. Add ginger, garlic and chilli and cook for 5-6 minutes over a medium heat. Stir in the ground spices and chilli flakes (if using) and cook for another minute.
4. Add Manjits Curry Masala Paste and cook through for 5 minutes.
5. Add the tomatoes and simmer for 10 minutes (add a splash of water if it looks dry) and continue to cook until the tomatoes break down and become slightly mushy.
6. Stir in the coconut cream and bring back to a fast simmer, then season with salt and pepper.
7. Squeeze over the lime (add zest to the sauce too for an extra kick of flavour).
8. Simmer for 5 minutes more until the sauce has thickened.
9. Gently place the fish in the sauce and rest the lid loosely on top (we want the steam to escape).
10. Cook over a medium-low heat for a few minutes (depending on the thickness of your fish) until the fish is cooked through and opaque.
11. Sprinkle scattered with chopped coriander leaves with plain basmati rice and extra lime wedges.

BALMAIN'S MOST POPULAR DISH

Balmain Bug Curry

A RECIPE FROM VARUN

Nowhere in India do we see Balmain bugs! We are so lucky to be in Australia surrounded by wonderful fresh seafood that we can play with and incorporate in our delicious cuisine. The Balmain bug curry is not overpowering; you can still taste the beautiful, sweet meat of the crustacean, and at the same time relish it with the smooth and creamy coconut sauce.

MANJITS AND THE TANDOOR OF SECRETS

Balmain Bug Curry

INGREDIENTS

	Balmain bug meat or fresh Balmain bugs shelled
3	Fried long red chillies—don't use the fresh ones for this!
¼ cup	Vegetable oil
1 tablespoon	Lime juice
½ teaspoon	Fenugreek seeds
½	Red onion, sliced very thinly
2 tablespoons	Manjits Curry Masala Sauce
2 tablespoons	Finely grated ginger paste (or a 7cm piece of ginger peeled and shredded)
4	Garlic cloves, finely chopped
1 tablespoon	Black mustard seeds
A handful	Fresh curry leaves
3 tablespoons	Ground turmeric
2 large	Roma tomatoes, roughly chopped
1 375ml can	Coconut cream
50 grams	Tamarind pulp, soaked in boiling water
Lime	Wedges to serve

BALMAIN'S MOST POPULAR DISH

METHOD

1. Strain tamarind through a sieve into a bowl, pressing to extract pulp (discard the seed). Set it aside and let it rest.
2. Heat oil in a large frying pan (that has a heavy base) over low heat.
3. Add in the mustard seeds and sauté until the seeds crackle. This will happen in about 20-30 seconds.
4. Add the chilli and the fenugreek seeds and cook until chillies brown. This should take about 20 seconds or so.
5. Bump up the heat to medium then add the onion and stir until soft and translucent.
6. Add in the ginger and the garlic and cook until aromatic and the house smells fantastic!
7. Stir in the Manjits curry base paste as well as the curry leaves and turmeric, stirring in for about 2 minutes. You will see the colour change. That's a good thing!
8. Add the tomato in and cook until soft. Should take about 3-4 minutes.
9. Stir through coconut cream and tamarind that you made in step 1.
10. Season to taste with sea salt and a touch of white pepper.
11. Stir pieces of the bug meat through sauce, cover and simmer over medium heat until just cooked through (12 minutes or so).
12. Turn off the heat and add a splash of lime juice.
13. Serve with lime wedges.
14. This dish is best enjoyed with steaming hot basmati rice. NOT roti or bread!

SOMETHING GENTLER

Lamb Korma

A RECIPE FROM ASH

Deep initially presented this dish to me as "butter chicken but nuttier and less tomato-y." This describes it perfectly. Too often I find myself at Manjits with my typical Aussie mates ordering 'Butter Chicken'. Every time I suggest trying a lighter, Korma instead. When they do, they too love the fragrant dish, and every time Varun tells me they are the two "whitest" dishes he can make.

MANJITS AND THE TANDOOR OF SECRETS

Lamb Korma

INGREDIENTS

4 tablespoons	Grapeseed oil
1 tablespoon	Cumin seeds
5	Red onions finely chopped
2 teaspoons	Salt
2 tablespoons	Fresh ginger minced
2 tablespoons	Fresh garlic minced
2 teaspoons	Cumin powder
2 teaspoons	Coriander powder
2 teaspoons	Turmeric
1 teaspoon	Kashmiri chilli powder
3 tablespoons	Tomato puree
3 tablespoons	Fresh cream
1	Fresh tomato cut into small cubes
1 kg	Leg of lamb cubed into small pieces (try to get ones with a bit of bone as it carries flavour)
1 litre	Hot water from the kettle
5 tablespoons	Chopped coriander
2 teaspoons	Garam masala
1 tablespoon	Cashew nuts

SOMETHING GENTLER

METHOD

1. In a big saucepan, heat the oil on medium/high heat. When the pleasant aroma of cumin is present, add the onions and salt after adding the cumin seeds and allowing them to sear. The onions should be cooked for 8 to 10 minutes, or until they are caramelised and a rich brown colour.

2. Add the ginger and garlic and cook for a couple of minutes stirring continuously since the fibrous garlic and ginger tends to stick to the bottom of the pan. Reduce the heat to low and follow with cumin powder, coriander powder, Kashmiri chilli powder and turmeric then cook for around about 1 minute. You need to let the spices cook and start releasing their oils. It is imperative that you stir all the time to ensure the spices do not burn.

3. Add the tomato puree and fresh tomato and cook for 1-2 minutes. Increase the flame to medium then add 250ml of hot water and reduce the mixture again, this should take 4-5 minutes. Yes, it sounds weird but it will really help develop the flavours in your gravy.

4. Add the lamb and stir with the fragrant masala. Cook for 5-7 minutes stirring continuously.

5. Add 750ml of hot water from the kettle and stir thoroughly scraping down the sides for any caramelised masala residue. Put a lid on the pan, reduce the heat to medium/low and simmer for 30-35 minutes, stirring every 3-4 minutes.

6. Once the lamb has cooked, if you prefer to have a runnier sauce, add more water from the kettle and cook for 2-3 minutes. Lastly add the dollop of cream to give it that nice rich Korma flavour and stir through. Stir in the coriander and garam masala and garnish with cashew nuts on top. Serve with pilao rice, naan or roti.

SOMETHING SO GOOD

Bharrah Kebab

A RECIPE FROM ASH

No dish makes it more apparent that Indian food is really more about 'flavour' than 'spice', than Manjits signature Bharrah Kebab using lamb cutlets. They are marinated in a mix of red spices for a minimum of four hours and then charcoal grilled. Combined with the high quality lamb in Australia, the Bharrah Kebab are tender, smoky and delicious.

MANJITS AND THE TANDOOR OF SECRETS

Bharrah Kebab

INGREDIENTS

	Lamb cutlets (try to get them with a little bit of fat on them)
1 tablespoon	Red chilli powder
1½ tablespoons	Tandoori masala marinade
	Salt to taste
	Pepper to taste
2 tablespoons	Yogurt
2 heaped teaspoons	Garlic Paste
2 heaped teaspoons	Ginger Paste
1 teaspoon	Lemon juice
1 teaspoon	Garam masala

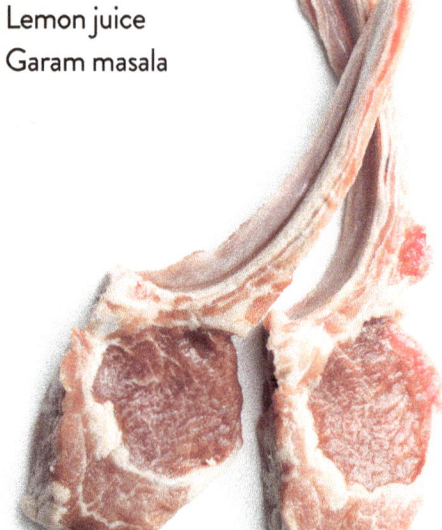

SOMETHING SO GOOD

METHOD

1. Combine all marinade ingredients (Chilli powder, salt, pepper, yogurt, garlic paste, ginger paste, garam masala and lemon juice) into a large bowl.
2. Mix well and add in the lamb cutlets in the same bowl, use your hands to coat the cutlets well and evenly.
3. Let the meat marinate for minimum 4 hours (preferably overnight) in the fridge. This is a very important step!
4. Cook on a charcoal grill or BBQ for about 15 minutes on both sides for well cooked meat.
5. Serve with thinly sliced red onions and a wedge of lemon.

NOTES

You can also add a little cream to the marinade to give it a bit of a richer flavour.

While the meat cooks on the grill you can brush it with a little butter on either side to avoid drying out.

If you're BBQ-ing, you need the BBQ to be really, really hot to sear the meat and lock the juices within. Then move the cutlets to a 'cooler' part to really cook them. Allow about 10-15 minutes per side.

MANJIT'S FAVOURITE

Goat Shoulder Curry

A RECIPE FROM MANJIT

I grew up with the ritual of Sunday Mutton Curry made from goat, often prepared by my dad in his pajamas. Sunday Mutton Curry is a Punjabi family's Sunday ritual. While we more commonly refer to mutton as lamb in Australia, it is goat in India. The preparation is rustic, not overly spiced and the meat doesn't need long hours of marination.

You can prepare it an Instapot/electric pressure cooker or in a regular pressure cooker. I however prefer slow cooking it in my casserole if I'm cooking for the kids. I have found that slow cooking mutton curry enhances the flavor of the meat and brings out that rich colour.

Simmer slowly in a heavy pot until the meat just falls off the bones and the entire house is filled with rich aromatic flavor of mutton and spices.

Secretly, I think dad enjoyed making it as much as we enjoyed eating it!

MANJITS AND THE TANDOOR OF SECRETS

Goat Shoulder Curry

INGREDIENTS

700 grams	Goat
4 medium sized	Chopped onion
2 tablespoons	Ginger
2 tablespoons	Garlic paste
2	Tomato puree
3 stems	Chopped green coriander leaves
2 tablespoons	Manjits Masala Curry Sauce

THE SPICES

2	Black cardamoms
3	Green cardamoms
1 inch	Cinnamon stick
4	Whole dry red chillies
2 tablespoons	Garam masala powder
2 tablespoons	Ground red chilli powder
1 tablespoon	Ground turmeric powder
5 tablespoons	Mustard oil
3 tablespoons	Ghee
1 tablespoon	Coriander powder
½ tablespoon	Cumin powder
½ bowl	Yogurt
1 tablespoon	Meat masala powder
4-5 Small	Cloves
2	Bay leaves
½ tablespoon	Cumin seeds
½ tablespoon	Whole black pepper

MANJIT'S FAVOURITE

METHOD

PREPARATION

1. Dry roast the black cardamom, bay leaf, green cardamom, cinnamon, red chilli, cumin, cloves. This will release the oils of the spices and add an amazing flavour. Then set aside.
2. Set the goat aside.

COOKING

3. Heat the thick bottomed pan , add mustard oil and put on medium heat and add the ghee.
4. Add black cardamom, bay leaf, green cardamom, cinnamon, red chilli, cumin, cloves that you dry roasted prior and wait till it starts to crackle. Cook for 1-2 minutes.
5. Add chopped onion and sauté until the edges become slightly golden.
6. Add ginger garlic paste and sauté it for 7 to 8 minutes on a low flame. This is so the garlic does not burn.
7. Add turmeric powder, red chilli powder, cumin powder, coriander powder, garam masala powder, a pinch of salt to taste, tomato puree and mix it thoroughly on a lower flame. You will find the colour of the curry changes to golden.
8. Add goat and sauté it for 10 minutes on high flame, without the lid to seal in the meat.
9. Add the Manjits masala curry sauce, cover and cook for 15 minutes on lower flame.
10. When the oil starts to separate from the masala base, add yogurt and a splash of water. Mix it well and cover and cook for 15 minutes or until the meat becomes tender.
11. Add some meat masala and chopped coriander leaves and mix it properly.
12. Ask mum to make some fresh chapati and... **Enjoy!**

KAWAL'S FAVOURITE

Fish Amritsari

A RECIPE FROM KAWAL

When I travelled in India, paying homage to the sacred Golden Temple was a rite of passage. It is a place people travel to from all around the world to pay respect, and to find grace and the meaning of life. No other place has attained so much peace, quiet and serenity. Outside the streets of Amritsar, the hustle and bustle of food vendors are prominent, and they do a roaring trade. By far the most popular item on the menu is Fish Amritsari.

MANJITS AND THE TANDOOR OF SECRETS

Fish Amritsari

INGREDIENTS

4cm piece	Finely grated ginger (about 20g)
1	Crushed garlic clove (use the fresh stuff!)
2 teaspoons	Sunflower oil, plus extra to deep-fry
800g	Skinless soft white fillets, pin-boned. I like ocean perch or flathead
Pinch	Chaat masala
	Lemon wedges, to serve

FOR THE GREEN CHUTNEY

½ bunch	Mint leaves
½ bunch	Coriander leaves
2	Long green chillies, chopped and deseeded
1	Medium red onion, chopped
½ tablespoon	Caster sugar
¼ tablespoon	Ground cumin
	Juice of 1 lime

FOR THE CHICKPEA BATTER

⅔ cup	Chickpea flour (besan)
¼ cup	Cornflour
3 tablespoons	Ground turmeric
200ml	Sparkling mineral or soda water super chilled

KAWAL'S FAVOURITE

METHOD

1. Combine ginger, garlic and oil in a bowl, then rub all over the fish to coat. Cover and chill for 15 minutes to marinate.
2. For the green chutney, place all the ingredients in a small food processor and pulse until finely chopped. Super easy!
3. For the chickpea batter, combine the chickpea flour, cornflour and turmeric in a bowl. Season, then whisk in sparkling water until smooth (batter should be the consistency of thin cream).
4. Half-fill a deep-fryer or large pan with sunflower oil and heat to 190°C.
5. Coat fish in the batter, then carefully add to the hot oil. Fry, turning halfway, for 2-3 minutes until golden and crisp. Remove with a slotted spoon and drain on paper towel.
6. Sprinkle fish with chaat masala and serve immediately with lemon and chutney.
7. You will love this. You have now found the meaning of life.

DEEP'S FAVOURITE

Yellow Dal

A RECIPE FROM DEEP

In my teens, when I once had friends over for dinner, I tried to make chicken curry to show off my skills as a Master Chef of Indian Cuisine. I failed miserably… leaving me in an embarrassing situation. So, what does a young, single, Indian-Aussie boy who's trying to show off his culinary skills do in the middle of the night to entertain a crowd? He makes the simplest dish that's guaranteed to put a smile on everyone's face! Dal!

Yellow Dal

INGREDIENTS

FOR THE DAL

½ cup	Red lentils (masoor dal)
½ cup	Yellow lentils (moong dal)
1 tablespoon	Oil
1 teaspoon	Garlic paste
1 teaspoon	Ginger paste
½ teaspoon	Turmeric powder
Salt to taste	

FOR TEMPORING

2 tablespoons	Ghee
½ small	Onion sliced (optional)
4	Garlic cloves sliced
2	Whole red chilli (dried)
1 teaspoon	Cumin seeds
	Coriander leaves for garnish

DEEP'S FAVOURITE

METHOD

1. Measure out the red lentils and yellow lentils and wash them. Usually, they don't need to be soaked because they cook quickly, but soak them for a couple of minutes till you gather the rest of the ingredients.
2. Heat 2 tablespoons of ghee in a large pan and add in the onion, garlic paste, ginger paste and turmeric powder. Sauté for a minute and then add the lentils along with salt. Add water, stir through and bring to a boil.
3. Once the water comes to the boil, put heat to low and cook for about 15 minutes till lentils are soft. If using a pressure cooker this will take 2 minutes. At this point, use a whisk or a wooden spoon to mix the lentils vigorously. This mashes the lentils creating a thick chunky stew. Add more water if desired, or just cook it for a few minutes if a thicker gravy is preferred.
4. For temporing, heat the oil in a small frying pan or small wok a few minutes before the lentils have finished cooking. Add the sliced onions fry till light golden. The garlic cloves are then added and sautéed for one minute, or until they are golden brown. Then add the cumin seeds after the whole red chillies. Cook for about 30-60 seconds till the cumin and red chillies change colour and release their aroma.

Carefully pour the tempering mixture over the lentils (including the oil) and mix through. Serve with rice, roti, chapati or naan.

NOTES

The amount of water used in a dal recipe depends on personal preference. Adjust depending on how you are going to eat the dal. If eating with roti, add less water and make it thicker and stew-like. If eating with rice, add more water to make it more liquid which coats the rice better.

VARUN'S FAVOURITE

Duck Curry

A RECIPE FROM VARUN

While Butter Chicken is a contested space between traditional and new ideas, so is duck curry. Duck is not a traditional protein for Indian cooking. However, I thought it was worth trying, while my dad was against it. You're not likely to find a recipe for Duck Curry anywhere else, so please do give it a try and decide for yourself what side of the old vs new debate you're on!

Duck Curry

INGREDIENTS

WET SPICE PASTE

2 tablespoons	Vegetable oil
2 teaspoons	Fennel seeds
2 teaspoons	Cumin seeds
3	Fresh green chillies broken in half
2 teaspoons	White poppy seeds
10	Raw cashew nuts
7	Garlic cloves crushed
2 tablespoons	Roasted Bengal gram (split)
1½ inch	Ginger crushed
60 gms	Fresh grated coconut

FOR THE CURRY

	Duck – breast and legs
3-4 tablespoons	Vegetable oil
5 cm	Cinnamon bark
4	Green cardamon pods
1 large	Onion finely chopped
½ teaspoon	Turmeric powder
2-3 sprigs	Curry leaves
2 large	Ripe tomatoes pureed
2 teaspoons	Red chilli powder
	Salt to season

VARUN'S FAVOURITE

METHOD

TO PREPARE THE WET SPICE PASTE

1. Heat oil in a large pan and add the cumin, fennel seeds and green chillies. Then add the poppy seeds, cashews and garlic; sauté for a few seconds until the garlic starts to brown on the edges.
2. Next add the Bengal gram, coconut and ginger. Mix well and sauté for a minute or two till the coconut turns a little toasty but not too brown.
3. Remove from heat and allow to cool thoroughly. Throw it in a blender with just enough water to get a wet paste.

NOW... TO MAKE THE CURRY

4. Heat the remaining oil in a large wok or kadhai. Add the cinnamon and cardamon followed by the onion. Sauté till the chopped onion is softened and turns light brown.
5. Next add the turmeric powder, chilli powder and curry leaves. Mix to combine.
6. Add the tomato puree and season with salt. Cook on medium heat till the mixture comes together and you can notice oil appearing at the sides of the mixture.
7. Next add the wet spice paste and mix well to combine. Sauté for about 5-6 minutes on low to medium heat stirring continuously.
8. Add the duck; mix well and cook for 1-2 minutes. Then add 1-2 cups of water (depending on how much gravy you prefer) and bring to the boil. Turn down the heat and simmer gently till the duck pieces have cooked perfectly and the gravy has thickened. The time for this will depend on the size of the duck pieces you are using. Taste and season with salt if necessary. Allow to sit for at least 30 minutes before serving.

SOMETHING TO FINISH

Dhokla

A RECIPE FROM KAWAL

My love for food from the Gujarat region,
on the western coast of India,
came when my son Deep organised
Gujarati weddings at Concord.
Their menus are always full of so many
different textures and tastes compared
with our Punjabi cuisine. I would
always grab some Dhokla, a savoury
steam cake, from the function
and have it as a healthy snack with my
chai in the afternoon.

MANJITS AND THE TANDOOR OF SECRETS

Dhokla

INGREDIENTS

2 cups	Red Gram (chickpea flour)
3	Green chillies
½ cup	Greek yoghurt
2 cups	Rice
2cm piece	Ginger
A pinch	Salt
½ teaspoon	Hing
½ teaspoon	Mustard seeds
10	Curry leaves
¼ cup	Olive oil

SOMETHING TO FINISH

METHOD

1. Soak the Red Gram and rice overnight in cold water.
2. Next day, mix to a batter adding some of the water used to soak if required.
3. Separately, mix the chillies, ginger, hing, and salt to taste and stir through with yoghurt. Add to the gram and rice batter.
3. Once the mixture has been combined ,place into a small flat bowl and steam for 15 minutes or so until a soft spongy texture.
4. Finish by heating oil and adding the mustard seeds, and curry leaves. The seeds and leaves must pop and spit to release the oil. Pour this hot mixture evenly on top of the sponge cake.
5. Slice into desired shape or size and enjoy hot or cold.

SOMETHING TO FINISH

Shahi Tukda

A RECIPE FROM MANJIT

One of my favourite things is making desserts. However, if deserts are too sweet then they have a sickly sort of effect. After a big dinner, or even an afternoon snack, I've always enjoyed making this scrumptious sweet dish. Surprisingly we have incorporated it into our events where some of our non-Indian clients have tasted it and described it as the Indian version of a bread and butter pudding!

MANJITS AND THE TANDOOR OF SECRETS

Shahi Tukda

INGREDIENTS

10 slices	White bread
5 cups	Full cream milk. As creamy as possible, it will make a massive difference
2 cups	Ghee for deep-frying
1 tablespoon	Milk powder
1 tablespoon	Condensed milk
15 to 18 strands	Saffron
1 teaspoon	Rose water
2 tablespoon	Pistachios - blanched and sliced
2 tablespoons	Dry fruits chopped for garnishing
½ cup	White sugar
1 sliver	Silver or gold leaf for garnish

SOMETHING TO FINISH

METHOD

1. Slice off the crust and cut each bread slice into a round shape with a cookie cutter.
2. Heat the ghee in a pan and shallow-fry the bread pieces for about a minute, turn over and fry about a minute more or until light brown and crisp then drain on absorbent paper towel to remove the excess grease. **DO NOT BURN THE GHEE**
3. Place the milk in a saucepan and start to simmer.
4. When you see the cream floating on top, use a spatula to gently move the cream layer towards the side of the pan so that it sticks to the side of the pan.
5. Keep on simmering the milk like this and collecting the cream layer on the sides. The more you do this the more it will get thicker and reduce to half. In other words… better!
6. Add pistachios and saffron.
7. Add sugar and continue to simmer for 5 minutes, stirring continuously.
8. Remove from flame, add rose water and chill it in the fridge for about 30 minutes.
9. Gently put bread pieces on a serving dish, and pour chilled, reduced milk over the bread pieces.
10. Apply silver leaf, and top with dry fruits.
11. Best served chilled… like my son Deep!

SOMETHING TO FINISH

Gulab Jamun

A RECIPE FROM VARUN

Back in the 1980s,
the way mum and dad described
Gulab Jamuns on the restaurant
menu was: "ping pong balls
soaked in a sweet cardamon syrup".
I'm sure that a lot of our customers
didn't know what the dish was,
but I think they all liked the concept
of eating "ping pong" balls!

MANJITS AND THE TANDOOR OF SECRETS

Gulab Jamun

INGREDIENTS

FOR THE JAMUNS

1 cup	Grated khoya / mawa
⅓ cup	Plain flour / maida
½ cup	Water (approximately)
A pinch	Salt
	Oil or ghee to deep fry

FOR THE SYRUP

2½ cups	Sugar
1 cup	Water
3–4 pods	Cardamon, crushed
2 drops	Rose water
A few strands	Saffron

SOMETHING TO FINISH

METHOD

1. Mix the grated khoya with the flour and salt. If using store-bought khoya, this mixture will be quite dry. If using home made khoya, it will be moist, so you need less water for the next step.
2. Add sufficient water (I use around ½ cup) and form a stiff dough. It shouldn't be sticky. If it is, add a bit more flour and incorporate without having to knead it too much.
   Note: *The addition of the water to the khoya and flour mix depends upon the texture of the khoya. If it is moist then less water is needed. You can add a pinch of cardamon powder to this as well.*
3. Make into small marble-sized balls. Remember to start small because the jamuns will expand on frying and on soaking in the sugar syrup. You don't have to make the balls super smooth, just into small circles of even sizes.
4. Heat oil to just short of smoking point and gently add the dough balls one-by-one. Don't overcrowd the dough balls, fry a few at a time. This also ensures that the oil temperature doesn't drop too much while frying.
5. Fry all the jamuns until golden brown on medium heat, remove with a slotted spoon, and set aside.
6. To make the syrup mix the water and sugar, and set on a medium-low flame. Stir until the sugar has dissolved completely and the mixture comes to a very slow boil. Add the crushed cardamon pods, saffron and rose water.
7. Let the sugar syrup cool for about 5 minutes only and then dunk in the fried jamuns, partially close the pan and let the jamuns soak in the syrup for at least 3-4 hours before serving. It can be served hot, cold or room temperature depending on preference.

Extras (The Basics)

EXTRAS

Masala Curry Sauce

A RECIPE FROM VARUN

A lot of Manjits curries are based on the Manjits master curry sauce.

MANJITS AND THE TANDOOR OF SECRETS

Masala Curry Sauce

INGREDIENTS

15	White onions sliced
400ml	Vegetable oil (do not use olive oil)
200 grams	Minced garlic
200 grams	Minced ginger
5 whole	Green chillies blended together
20	Tomatoes finely chopped
3 tablespoons	Tomato paste
1 tablespoon	Garam masala
½ tablespoon	Cumin
½ tablespoon	Coriander powder
1 tablespoon	Smoked paprika
¼ teaspoon	Mace
½ tablespoon	Cardamom powder
1 tablespoon	Deggi Mirch (a blend of red capsicum and red chillies)
½ tablespoon	White pepper
1 tablespoon	Turmeric powder
1 tablespoon	Cloves
1 litre	Water

EXTRAS

METHOD

1. Use a big pot with a thick base and add the oil till warm.
2. Add the onions and let them become translucent and caramelised. Do this on a low and slow heat, cooking for a minimum of 30 minutes.
3. Add the garlic, ginger, and minced chillies and allow them to cook through.
4. Add 1 litre of water with turmeric which turns the mixture a yellowish tinge.
5. Add in the tomatoes and all the spices and let simmer for another 30 minutes.
6. Once slightly cooled, add the tomato paste and use a stick blender to puree the mixture in the pot.
Be aware of the heat and splatter that may come from this.
7. Once cool, the sauce can be used for nearly all of the recipes in this book and can stored for two weeks under a layer of oil.
8. It's a long process, but batch making will make life much easier.

Weights and Measures

Measuring cups and spoons vary slightly from country-to-country. Although the differences are not generally enough to significantly affect a recipe, here is what we base our measurements on.
All cup and spoon measures are level.

One Australian cup = 250 ml or 8 fl oz
One Australian tablespoon = 20 ml or 4 teaspoons
One Australian teaspoon = 5 ml

The most accurate way to measure dry ingredients is to weigh them. But the reality is most household kitchens use a cup or some other form of measurement. The important thing is to make sure the dry ingredient is loosely leveled; never pack it down unless a recipe says "firmly packed" or similar.

¼ cup = 60 ml or 2 fl oz
⅓ cup = 80 ml or 2½ fl oz
½ cup = 125 ml or 4 fl oz
1 cup = 250 ml or 8 fl oz

15g = ½ oz
30g = 1 oz
60g = 2 oz
125g = 4 oz or ¼ lb
250g = 8 oz or ½ lb
500g = 16 oz or 1 lb

Acknowledgements

Thank you to the Gujrals
- Manjit, Kawal, Deep and Varun -
for sparing me the time to put together
this glimpse into their culture,
their lives and their family story.
Thanks also to Ash Reynolds for the
insights and anecdotes. I have greatly
enjoyed getting to know all of you.

This wouldn't be here without my publisher, **Bonita Mersiades**, who not only agreed to take a punt on a book like this from a former sports hack, but who kept me focused on this wonderful project when I was going through a rough patch personally. I also have a deep appreciation to **Leslie Priestley** for his beautiful design work. A book with recipes would be nothing without his magic, as well as the photography which brings the food to life.

A shout-out to my four children, all of whom I love dearly. And finally, love and thanks to **Kellie McVie** who came into my life last year and has been a joy, an inspiration, and a great reason to be alive!

About the Author

Michael Cain was a senior journalist for Channel 10 in Sydney until September 2020. He now works as a freelance journalist.

He was the recipient of the Sports Australia Best Reporting of an Issue in Sport in the 2022 Sports Media Awards, along with colleagues from the Daily Telegraph and SBS-TV. He is the producer and writer of the 'Mark Viduka Uncovered' broadcast on ESPN.

Michael lives in Newcastle, Australia, and has four children.

Manjits and the Tandoor of Secrets is his first book.

PEPPER PRESS

www.pepperpress.com.au

www.ingramcontent.com/pod-product-compliance
Lightning Source LLC
Chambersburg PA
CBHW051315110526
44590CB00031B/4367